Jesus Hates Religion foc⸍ ⸍⸍⸍⸍⸍⸍⸍⸍
a relationship with Chri⸍⸍ ⸍⸍⸍⸍ ⸍⸍ ⸍⸍⸍⸍⸍⸍, ⸍⸍⸍⸍,
feelings of inferiority. The man-made path of religion
has no place in the heart of the Christ follower, and
Alex Himaya brings this concept to life.

Craig Groeschel
Senior Pastor of LifeChurch.tv
Author of *The Christian Atheist*

I wish I could tell you this is a book you can't put down,
but it's not. It's a book you may have to put down. In
fact, at times you might even want to throw it away or
punch it. But let the radical message of Jesus within
these pages make its claim, and the death of your religion will blossom into true life in Jesus.

Dr. Jerry Gillis
Lead Pastor at The Chapel at CrossPoint
Buffalo, New York

The single most important decision a person will ever
make concerns their relationship with Jesus Christ.
Alex reminds us that it is not about rules or religion,
but an intimate relationship.

Dr. Johnny Hunt
Pastor at First Baptist Church
Woodstock, Georgia

JESUS

hates

RELIGION

ALEX HIMAYA

>> *Finding* **GRACE** *in a*
Works-Driven Culture >>

JESUS

hates

RELIGION

B&H
PUBLISHING GROUP
Nashville, Tennessee

Published by B&H Publishing Group
Nashville, Tennessee

Dewey Decimal Classification: 234.1
Subject Heading: RELIGION \ GRACE (THEOLOGY) \
CHRISTIAN LIFE

1 2 3 4 5 6 7 • 18 17 16 15 14

To my four sweet children, Katherine, Elijah,
Benjamin, and Lemley, you have brought me more joy,
laughter, and grace than you will ever know.
May your lives be filled with the sweet grace of Jesus!

Acknowledgments

Thanks be to my Lord and Savior Jesus Christ, you have shown me unimaginable grace and rescued me from the grips of religion.

To Meredith, my beautiful wife. You are truly my best friend and soul mate.

Special thanks to my parents, Drs. Mack and JoAnn Himaya for pushing me to more than I ever thought possible; to Lonita Beaty, Saundra Powell, and Sheryl Keck for doing the hard work of making my thoughts legible; and to the people of theChurch.at for being the greatest grace place I know of!

Contents

Foreword

"Apart from Me, you can do nothing."

—Jesus

It seems, maybe, we have forgotten that Jesus said we can do nothing without Him. Nothing.

That is why I am so grateful for a book like this—a book about Jesus. Not another dead book about religion, but one about the only Source of life that exists. Simply put, there is no definition of life apart from Jesus—He said He is life Himself. It seems, though, we act as if we can do this "Christian life thing" on our own—just work a little harder, have a bit more discipline than the next guy, etc. It's as if we think, fundamentally, Christianity is about our effort to be like Jesus.

It's not. That's the opposite of good news. In fact, it's horrible news—have you ever tried it? C. S. Lewis, in his classic work *Mere Christianity*, got it right: "No man knows how bad he is till he has tried very hard to be good."[1] Christianity is not about our effort to be like Jesus; it is Jesus' effort to be Himself in us. Alex Himaya gives you an honest and compelling look at how religion—man-made attempts to get to God—will fail you every time. And that's why Jesus hates religion—because it keeps you from Him.

As Leonard Sweet and Frank Viola point out in *Jesus Manifesto*, Jesus didn't even try to live His life on this earth by His own power (religion). Jesus said, "Most assuredly, I say to you, the Son can do nothing of Himself" (John 5:19 NKJV), and in another place He said, "I can of Myself do nothing" (John 5:30 NKJV). So, since Jesus could do nothing of Himself, what did He do? He said it this way, "Whatever the Father does the Son also does," and again, "I do nothing on my own but speak just what the Father has taught me" (John 5:19; 8:28 NIV). And finally, "Don't you believe that I am in the Father, and that the Father is in me? The words I say to you are not just my own. Rather, it is the Father, living in me, who is doing his work" (John 14:10 NIV).

Jesus lived His life through the indwelling of the Father. So do you really think that Jesus is going to tell us to live our lives any differently—that somehow we should live our lives on our own, in our own strength, and just try to copy Jesus? Are we to think that religion, which wasn't good enough for Jesus, is somehow good enough for us? Good luck—that is the recipe for abject failure. Trying to be like Christ is not only hard; it is impossible. Only Christ can be like Christ. And that's the point. He indwells us. He lives in us. And He wants to live His life out through us.

We could take all the great information from all of the books on the best-seller list and put it all into practice. We could have better parenting skills, better communication in marriage, and all other kinds of self-help; but, in the end, apart from Jesus, we really can do nothing. When the life of Jesus is being lived out in us, we will be better spouses, parents, and people because His life manifestly becomes bigger than ourselves; it becomes about Jesus and His power.

We need to step out of our "*you*-niverse of religion" and into Jesus' universe. Everything, and I mean everything, is for Him, through Him, in Him, and by Him. He must have preeminence. If we don't allow that, the alternative is not good: we begin to unknowingly drown in the pool of religious narcissism while thinking what great swimmers we are. The "*you*-niverse of religion" is nothing more than a black hole, but thankfully Alex hasn't written a book on religion. He has written about the only One who really matters—the all-sufficient Jesus who saves us from our sins, our mistakes, our very selves; and, yes, from our religion too.

Dr. Jerry Gillis
Lead Pastor at The Chapel at CrossPoint
Buffalo, New York

Introduction

Perhaps you picked up this book because you're appalled by the title and can't wait to tear this book apart. Or maybe the title caught your attention, and you enthusiastically agree because you've experienced religion at its worst.

I should probably state here that I am a pastor. Those of you who were already angry just blew a gasket. Keep reading.

I realize that being author of a book entitled *Jesus Hates Religion* puts me in a precarious situation. I am a pastor. My main source of income is from a church—a "religious institution." I have spent thousands of dollars and decades of my time learning from religious institutions. It seems crazy for me to state that Jesus hates something that is the core of who I am and what I do. However, I want to offer an unbiased view of God's thoughts about religion. Before you put this book back on the shelf, please allow me to share some of my life story with you.

Living and breathing religion, since I was a teenager, may seem like the perfect recipe for a biased view of religion; but in reality, it's been a backstage pass to see religion at its best and at its worst. Throughout my journey, I've found that many like to talk about the "worst" side of religion. People are comfortable discussing great religious leaders who have publicly been humiliated for their hypocrisy. Many are quick to condemn a person who has hurt others in the name of Jesus. And many more refuse to take personal responsibility for their daily actions, Monday through Saturday, hoping that people only judge them based on their display at church Sunday morning.

I am not comfortable pretending that these things don't happen. In fact, it makes me sick to see God so grossly misrepresented. Throughout my experience with religion, I have been acquainted with people who called themselves religious, yet used their religion to hurt, reject, and betray others. I've also seen those far from God use religion (and all that goes with it) as an excuse to stiff-arm God. And that's the reason I had to write this book.

I have been hurt by religious people.

I have been betrayed by religion.

I've studied the Bible and gotten to know God on a personal level. I've found that those so-called religions are not at all what the Bible teaches. In fact, most are a direct perversion of the true freedom God offers each person as a free gift.

My Pledge

Having said all that, here is my pledge to you:

I promise this book will not be filled exclusively with my spin on what the Bible says.

I will lay before you what the Bible has to say and let you choose for yourself.

I will go into depth exploiting the most common misinformation people equate with religion and compare it to what the Bible actually teaches.

Your Pledge

We all know the saying, "It takes two to tango." In order for this partnership to work, I need you to promise you won't leave me dancing alone. You as the reader also have a part to play.

Your part is two-fold. Number one, as you read this book, commit to quiet your mind and set aside all of the teachings you have heard that relate to God. I know for some of you this means looking past years and years, perhaps even a lifetime, of teachings and instructions that have shaped your beliefs about who He is. For others of you, it means letting go of memories that have wounded and scarred your heart and have affected every decision you've made since.

I know what I'm asking isn't easy, but if you make the pledge to listen only to the Bible, you may just find the hope and the love that you've been yearning for all of these years.

Number two, you need to read the Bible for yourself. It would be hypocritical for me to tell you that reading my book will answer all of your questions. I can't and I won't promise you that. I can promise that if you read the Bible, just the Bible, you will find the hope and the answers you've been looking for. When a verse is quoted in this book, find it in your own Bible. Read the verses surrounding that verse. Read the entire chapter. Read the entire book. The Bible will not contradict itself, so use the other verses to validate and interpret what you're reading.

I would encourage you to choose the translation you're most comfortable with. I don't necessarily mean the one you or your family has always read. Choose a version you can read and understand without having to consult a dictionary, thesaurus, and college professor to translate each sentence. If you don't know which version to begin with, I recommend the *New Living Translation*.

Most of the verses I reference in this book come from that version of the Bible because, for me, it's one of the easiest to follow and understand.

Once you've set aside your previous perceptions of God and have your Bible, then you're ready to learn about a journey that, more than likely, religion has not been able to offer you. Stick with me. This book isn't going to neatly fit into any "religion" category at your local bookstore, and I'm perfectly fine with that.

Chapter One

Abandoned by Religion

Growing up, religion was not really a predominant part of my family's life, which created a curiosity in me; so, I, honestly, tried it all—confirmation, catechism, becoming an altar boy, memorizing the Lord's Prayer, meeting early with my priest before church to pray over the bread and wine for communion, carrying the cross during worship services, attending youth camps, the works. I've been a Coptic, a Catholic, an Episcopalian, and a Baptist.

My dad is full-blooded Egyptian, born and raised in Cairo. My mom was raised in the hills of Fletcher, North Carolina. Talk about crazy family reunions! I have full-blooded Arab cousins on one side, who dress to impress at every social event [think prom], and a cousin from the other side of my family, who built all of his furniture out of PVC pipe. Despite being Egyptian, my dad wasn't Muslim as some would assume. He was Coptic, which is similar to Catholicism, but with a lot more tradition. It is the Orthodox Christian Church of Egypt.

Since Coptics aren't as common in America, my family attended an Episcopal church—sort of. We were there for the important religious holidays, but that was about it. I made up for my lack of church attendance by attending an all-boys Catholic high school. During my junior year, the school switched to coed for which we were all grateful.

I played the religion game throughout my teenage years, but the first time I started to doubt the validity of the rules—the dos and don'ts I was expected to follow—was in junior high. Even though I participated in every religious duty I was eligible for at that age, I still felt something was missing. So I began a double life. When I was in church, I was dressed in my finest and my behavior stood as a shining example for all the younger boys. However, when I wasn't at church, I was searching for answers in the wrong places. The moment I realized my experience of being immersed in religion had only left me empty and discouraged, I walked away.

It wasn't the shortcut to peace and happiness I was anticipating. Why? I'm human. I make mistakes. Many times I strayed from the path. After graduation, I went to a religious university, but my life still strayed down the wrong paths of religion and left me hoping beyond reason that things were going to magically work themselves out when I got older.

I don't hate religion because of what it did to me. I hate it because of what it didn't do. I hate what it has done to others. And most of all, I hate when it leaves out the truth about Jesus and what God has to offer. In fact, that's why Jesus hates religion too. It's missing all the good stuff.

The End of the Game

It took me many years, many mistakes, and many hurts before I came to the understanding and convictions that I embrace today. My own emptiness, accompanied by the disillusionment of my friends,, made me realize something wasn't right. There had to be a different answer. There had to be a better way. There had to be some good that came out of the Bible—otherwise why would its stories be repeated in so many cultures? Why would so many people still follow it thousands of years after it was written? Why would so many give their lives defending it?

I cleared my head and started from scratch. I put aside everything I had been taught about God, the

Bible, and religion. I decided to focus on one source—the Bible. I didn't want anyone else's opinions or interpretations tainting my experience. I wanted to know what the Bible said when someone else wasn't telling me what it said. I wanted to let the Bible tell me what the Bible says.

As I studied and searched the Scriptures, I found a plan and purpose that no one had shown me before. I found a way to God that didn't involve any good works, good behavior, or impossible dos and don'ts. I found that knowing, trusting, and following God had little to do with me and everything to do with God.

There was only one step that God required of me. Acceptance. As simple as accepting a present and claiming ownership, I found that my connection with God is a gift I choose to accept or reject.

That's it. No more. No less.

People have tried to add to or delete from that truth in their own search for God. And when humans add to or delete from the Bible, it's no longer truth.

We've all been hurt, and we've all hurt others. But I now understand that it wasn't God's design for us to experience all of this rejection and pain in the name of religion.

I can only begin to imagine the tears, the agony, and the betrayal that the readers of this book could list for me. It's not easy to trust in a God who sees all of this hurt happening; but let me show you what I've found in the Bible. More importantly, let me just show you the Bible, and let the Bible speak for itself.

The Beginning of Truth

I truly believe that with a little of your trust and time, this book could potentially point you to answers that religious people have been falling short to provide for thousands of years.

I believe there is a God—a good God, a God who loves and accepts you just as you are. I also believe that the truth about who He is has been severely tainted by religion and religious people. I'm not presuming I can change your mind, but I am offering you a voice that's willing to acknowledge the hurt that's resulted from religion, and I'm laying before you an open conversation about the why, the how, and the what God has to say about it.

Don't trust me. Trust God, and let Him speak for Himself.

Study Questions

1. How has religion impacted your life?

2. What are you expecting you'll find in the following pages?

3. What is or has been the foundation of truth in your life?

Chapter Two

Culture and Religion

When I began working on what was originally a sermon series, that I preached in 2009, that later evolved into this book, my church posted a billboard that simply stated, "www.jesushatesreligion.com." Immediately a flood of opinions ranging from curious support to extreme disgust filled the message board. Some people were compelled to weigh in with their definitions of the word *religion* and how it had either positively or negatively affected their lives. Others suggested outrage that a church, which they equated with religion, would put the name *Jesus* in the same sentence with *hate*.

Whatever statement is made about religion, it becomes a polarizing discussion. Feelings and conversations about religion occur at both ends of a very wide spectrum. On one end, you have people who won't even discuss religion; on the other end of the spectrum, you've got people going to war over it; and somewhere in the middle, you have people hurt and betrayed by the role religion played in their lives. Regardless, the things that people do and say in the name of *God* added to the things that people do and say in the name of *religion* is enough to fully fund entire news networks all over the globe.

Religion Defined

As I mentioned before, it appears contradictory to write this book as a pastor trying to explain why Jesus hates religion. The word *religion* occurs somewhere between five and seven times in the Bible depending on the translation. In *The Message* it appears 162 times. Do a search on the word *religion* in *The Message* on the Internet. About twenty-five occurrences in, you will get the message, so to speak. In almost all of them the connotation is negative. The one reference that is clearly presented in a positive light is James 1:27, which talks about pure religion that cares for widows and orphans.

Religion began in the garden of Eden, when Adam and Eve tried to make coverings for themselves out of fig leaves, a bloodless sacrifice. It continued with the offering of Cain in Genesis 4. These were the first man-made attempts to get back to God. So, as we begin on this journey, I feel it is vital that I give you my working definition of religion. The religion I am referring to, when I declare that Jesus hates religion, is a man-made path to God.

The Bible clearly lays out a design and plan for a perfect God to be able to have a relationship with an imperfect person. That plan is, by design, a path that only God could have made available to man. Man, in his imperfection, is not capable of creating a path that successfully reaches God.

Throughout history, well-meaning, intelligent, religious leaders have ignored their own human limitations; consequently, they have created a wealth of dead-end, stifling, and broken religions. When people choose to follow those dead-end journeys, they find themselves feeling damaged and betrayed. When this happens, most people blame God, which results in them moving farther and farther away from Him. What they don't realize is that God had nothing to do with that journey, and ultimately they miss out on the path He did create—a path of freedom, hope, and security.

Religious leaders will try to convince you their man-made path, typically a list of "dos" and "don'ts" they choose to adhere to, is the only way for God to be experienced. The result is usually a life filled with frustration and guilt, when that journey asks for more than it provides. Generally, a person who lives a life committed to religion will find himself on his deathbed, hoping he did enough to earn God's favor.

Fix-It Men

Religion is pride. It's a human being or a group of human beings looking at the distance between them and God, and then saying, "I can right this wrong." In other words, they believe there are ways they can be good enough—by filling their lives with love, purity, acts of kindness, social justice, etc.—to earn God's favor. They walk through life committed to avoiding predetermined "bad" things and to doing enough "good" things that they will somehow be guaranteed a seat in heaven. Ultimately, all of these little paths are arrogance because they're saying, "*I* can fix that."

But when you get away from all of the teachings, all of the preaching, all of the performers, and when you just read the Bible, you'll find one clear message: it's not about you being "good" enough . . . it's about God being enough. Period.

Religion Church

Since most people equate church with religion, it's important to identify what the Bible actually says is the purpose of the church. One of the purposes God intended for the church is community—a group of people, with a common purpose, doing life together. In Acts 2:42–47, the Bible describes the first New Testament church. The believers, who all held a common belief that Jesus was the Son of God and had been raised from the dead, came together, devoted themselves to the apostles' teaching, shared their lives with each other, and found encouragement and support.

As humans, we all desire community. In fact, that's why Starbucks is so successful: one of its core principles is to create a place where people can gather and converse. Starbucks has replaced the front porches and backyards of neighborhoods across America. People used to talk with their neighbors about what's going on in their lives. Today, people meet at a café to accomplish the same purpose.

The founder of Starbucks recognized a need for community, and he built an empire fulfilling that need. Outside of cafés, today's culture comes up short fulfilling people's needs for community. Perhaps that's why social networking became so popular so quickly. It fulfilled a need for community—a place where there were no strings attached and people could just do life with other people.

One of the reasons God created the church was to fulfill our need for community, yet people have twisted and perverted the church, to the point it has become a place for people to unite with like-minded believers, who ascribe to a common code of ethics. So, when I say that Jesus hates religion, I'm not saying that God hates the church. He loves the church. He created it! The church is the body of Christ and the bride of Christ. He hates the perversion of many churches that have added their own rules and standards to His genuine, honest, and simple offer of relationship.

> When I say that Jesus hates religion, I'm not saying that God hates the church. He loves the church. He created it! He hates the perversion of many churches that have added their own rules and standards to His genuine, honest, and simple offer of relationship.

Granted, today's culture generally defines *church* as a gathering of religious people, which makes me sick because that definition is missing so much. It's so far away from what God created and purposed for the church. As a pastor, my desire is to see the people who attend church transform from a gathering of religious people creating their own paths to God into a gathering of people who know and believe that without God nothing is possible.

I love the church. There's something very powerful in being a part of a community of Christ followers with a common purpose, and I believe there are many great churches that exist today. It is powerful when all of the people—from the pastor to the volunteers changing diapers in the nursery—are all striving toward the same purpose: a relationship with God, undefiled by man's dos and don'ts. The church is not equal to; it is greater than man-made religion.

Christians Aren't Allowed to Hate . . . Right?

After defining *religion* and *church*, it's important that I also discuss the relationship between Christians and hate. One incensed person who commented on the Jesus Hates Religion message board had this to say:

> Jesus is the opposite of hate. He's everything good and pure. I realize that a lot, if not all, organized religions have lost their way, but there's no hatred in Jesus.

Another upset person recommended the web address be changed to *www.JesusPrefersChristianUnity.com*. (Yeah, that would get about three hits.)

Rewind a minute. Let's start with what *hate* means. *Hate* is defined as having an "extreme dislike" of something. Since religion is a man-made path to God, then religion is a deviation from God's purpose and plan. God clearly states in the Bible that Jesus is the only way to heaven: "Jesus told him, 'I am the way, the truth, and the life. No one can come to the Father except through me'" (John 14:6).

If people, on their own, try to create ways to God, they are essentially saying they know better than God and their path is better than God's. That's pure arrogance, and what does the Bible say about arrogance?

> Human pride will be humbled,
> and human arrogance will be brought down.
> Only the LORD will be exalted
> on that day of judgment. (Isa. 2:17)

There's little room for debate that arrogance is something that God has an extreme dislike for. He hates it. It was pride that caused Lucifer to exalt himself and rebel against God's authority. Pride is what caused the fall of man, when Adam and Eve sinned in the garden of Eden. In fact, pride is one of the seven sins that God hates and are an abomination to Him. If we really stop to think about it, pride is at the root of most of the sin we commit. So if religion, at its core, is pride and arrogance, then one can make a strong argument that Jesus hates religion.

Jesus Wasn't a Religious Leader

Jesus was not just another great teacher. He was not just a motivational speaker. He certainly did not come to start a religion, nor did He come to this earth to lead people to create their own paths to finding God. In fact, He would've hated being given the title "religious leader." Jesus' purpose was to be *the* path to God—the *only* one.

Biblical Christianity is different from religion. Plain and simple, Christianity is a relationship with God—God's way. In Jesus' day, all of the religious leaders hated Christianity because it was not religious.

> In Jesus' day, all of the religious leaders hated Christianity because it was not religious.

It didn't follow a list of dos and don'ts. It was the anti-religion. Jesus welcomed anybody and everybody with open arms. He didn't discriminate against imperfect people. In fact, He chose to surround Himself with the very same people that the religious leaders condemned and shunned:

> Later, Levi held a banquet in his home with Jesus as the guest of honor. Many of Levi's fellow tax collectors and other guests also ate with them. But the Pharisees and their teachers of religious law complained bitterly to Jesus' disciples, "Why do you eat and drink with such scum?"
>
> Jesus answered them, "Healthy people don't need a doctor—sick people do. I have come to call not those who think they are righteous, but those who know they are sinners and need to repent." (Luke 5:29–32)

If religion is man making a path to God, Christianity is understanding the path is already made—through a relationship with Jesus. It's the only way.

Religion loses sight of the goal. Contrary to what most religious leaders would tell you, the focus of religion is the deeds that move you toward or away from the destination. The focus of religion is not God. The focus of religion is being good. But if you look at the word *good* and take out the letters *g-o-d,* you're left with something that looks a lot like a zero, and it is worth about that much too. Nothing. That's what good is without God. Nothing.

Choose Your Adventure

Christianity is not about being good. Good works have nothing to do with whether or not God accepts you. Yet religious leaders around the world are mobilizing armies of believers, who think that performing enough good works, which vary from religion to religion, is the only way for God to accept them.

One of the most common ways a religion is formed is when a person or a group of people read the Bible and decide to pick and choose the parts they like, and then, ignore the rest. Everyone loves to hear about God's forgiveness and mercy; yet because society has taught us to believe achievements validate our success, most find it hard to accept that a perfect God could have any love for an imperfect person who has done no good.

The Bible has a simple message. God loved us when we were imperfect and made a way to connect to Him, despite our imperfections. When this simple message has been altered or removed from the equation, what's left is a group of people trying to forge a path toward God. Some people never find a group, so they trek on alone. The result is a life bound by cynicism, guilt, disappointment, and hatred—which is so far away from the life and message of Jesus Christ. So far away.

Jesus came to accomplish something entirely different than that. Look at the words that He uses to describe His mission on earth: *seek, save, deliver, break, heal* (Luke 19:10; Matt. 6:13 (NIV); 8:7). Jesus stood against the bondage of religion, and Satan and the religious people of His day hated Him for it.

Jesus' purpose was never about conforming to this, that, and the other. His message was always about transformation. Jesus was never about what was forbidden; He was always about freedom.

> Jesus was never about what was forbidden; He was always about freedom.

Take a moment to step back and look at your experience with God. Evaluate your current path. Consider the paths you have followed. If you've been raised in a religious environment, give yourself a chance to sift through the opinions and teachings you've grown up with.

- Has your experience with God been about the "dos" and the "don'ts"?
- Are you on a path that was decided for you by people you trusted, but it feels more like bondage?
- Have you completely abandoned all paths because you've seen the end results, and you have no desire whatsoever to be a part of that?

- Have you been blinded by hurt and betrayal?
- Have you been crushed by "the church"?
- Have you lost all desire to even find a path?

Or are you on a path that God and God alone has created—a path you stepped onto naked and without anything to contribute? Has your walk with God been a constant reminder that without Him, none of this is possible?

> For my part, I am going to boast about nothing but the Cross of our Master, Jesus Christ. Because of that Cross, I have been crucified in relation to the world, set free from the stifling atmosphere of pleasing others and fitting into the little patterns that they dictate. Can't you see the central issue in all this? It is not what you and I do. . . . It is what God is doing, and he is creating something totally new, a free life! All who walk by this standard are the true Israel of God—his chosen people. (Gal. 6:14–16 *The Message*)

A Culture of Success

If you've been raised in today's culture, you have been bombarded with messages that indicate that your value is defined by successes and achievements. It begins from the moment your parents cheer your first steps and continues in the form of grades, pay scales, and material possessions. Over and over we are inundated with slogans like, "If at first you don't succeed, try, try again," "Pull yourself up by your own bootstraps," and "Practice makes perfect." Ultimately, the fruit of living in an achievement-based society is a high value on self-sufficiency. In fact, we honor it.

But God wants to see what it is we cannot accomplish, and then He wants us to accept it as a gift from Him. Culture has always dictated that we must have something to offer God, but God offers His achievements (achievements we are not capable of accomplishing without Him) to accept as our own. And as we dig further into what religion today has become, we'll see how culture has crept in and perverted our definition of religion from God's offer of relationship.

Study Questions

1. How do you define religion?

2. How was Jesus a "religious leader"? How was He not a "religious leader"?

3. How would you describe Jesus' mission here on earth?

Chapter Three

The Religion of Self

*I have seen churches that are more legalistic/
religious and ones that are less so. Trying to be honest and transparent with people is not weakening the
message of Christ. Admitting that we all fall short
is not lowering God's standards. We must admit
fault to accept forgiveness! I have never met an
unbeliever, or one who sits on the fence, who wants
to have a discussion about the law. Christ Himself
never approached people this way. We are victorious
through relationship, not religion.*

—B. [Excerpted from www.jesushates
religion.com message board]

Have you ever encountered a literal dead end
while driving your car? Your journey was all
mapped out, every turn and stop carefully

calculated, and yet you only got so far in your trip and found out the road you planned to take was closed. Just like that, your trip came to a dead stop, and you couldn't go farther because your vacation was facing a premature end. No matter how upset you were that the road was closed, it didn't change the fact that if you didn't choose another road, your journey was over. At that point you had to pick another route.

We'd agree, I'm sure, that dead ends are generally negative—like a dead end in your pay scale at work. You've put in more than what's asked of you, but your boss has frankly explained that while he/she appreciates you, you've reached the top in your department. Maybe it's a subject in school that no matter how many hours you dedicate to studying or how many dollars you pour into a tutor, you just can't pass that class. Maybe it's a dead end in a relationship, and you feel like you just can't move on. Maybe it's in your pursuit of God.

Dead ends are inevitable in life, but is that always a bad thing? What if dead ends could save your life? What if dead ends are imperative in developing a relationship with God? Ultimately, all paths to God will barrel recklessly into a dead end, including the path that God created. Man-made paths dead-end in failure. No matter how good the intentions of religious leaders, a man-made path to God will never reach its destination. On God's path, we crash into Him.

The path that God has created includes two dead ends. Each of us must hit these dead ends, face them, and deal with them before successfully entering a real relationship with God. The first dead end occurs *so that* you can enter a personal relationship with Him.

> No matter how good the intentions of religious leaders, a man-made path to God will never reach its destination. On God's path, we crash into Him.

At a key moment during the US Civil War, President Abraham Lincoln reluctantly signed a no furlough order. It broke his heart to keep the enlisted men of the Union from going home to see their loved ones, but their service in the battle was more important.

One soldier had made his way to Washington, D.C., to see the President and request an exemption. He wanted a furlough to see his dying wife at home, but he was not allowed in. He hung his head in sadness and left the White House. Outside he caught the eye of President Lincoln's son, Tad. Tad, who was less than ten years old during the US Civil War, was known to be a friend of many of the soldiers. He even had a special military uniform made in his size, and he wore it often around the capital.

When Tad saw this brokenhearted soldier, he ran up to him. "What's the matter, sir?" the young boy asked. The soldier looked down into Tad's eyes and explained, "My wife is dying and I wanted a furlough, but they won't allow me to see the President." "Very well," the little child replied. "You take my hand. I am President Lincoln's son and I will take you in to see him."

Leading him up the steps to the President's room, he passed by several guards who gave way to the young boy in his military dress. They regarded him with the same respect as his father. But once at the doors to the President's quarters, he was met with resistance. "The President is busy," the guard responded. But, little Tad would not be denied. He held tight to the soldier's hand.

Just then, the door opened and President Lincoln caught his young son's eye. "Father," he called out. "Tell this man to let me come in." Abraham Lincoln immediately stopped what he was doing and told the guard to let his son approach. After the boy explained the soldier's plight, the President stroked the hairs on his chin, looked at his boy, and then smiled deeply. He took up a pen and immediately signed an order of furlough, sending the soldier on his way home.[2]

Likewise, in order to gain access onto God's path, you must hit the first dead end—the dead end of self-trust. In order to move on, you must believe and confess, "*I* can't do this."

It's Not You—It's Me

How many of you have ever been in a relationship with someone that ended it using the classic line, "It's not you—it's me"?

When we hit a painful dead end while on our own path to God, we're forced to acknowledge the opposite—it's not me; it's all You. You, God, are the only right path for me.

The Bible is full of stories, not just for historical or entertainment purposes. Each story serves as a picture of one or more spiritual truths. God knew that just giving us His Word in list form would not connect with everyone. He included

> When we hit a painful dead end while on our own path to God, we're forced to acknowledge the opposite—it's not me; it's all You.

stories to serve as visual illustrations that people can parallel with their own life journeys and apply the truths inherent in those stories.

The idea of hitting God's dead end of self-trust is found in the story of the Israelites' escape from Egypt into the Promised Land. At the risk of this suddenly feeling "religious," I want to show you this story. Read on. It's good stuff.

Exodus, the second book of the Bible, is where this story begins. The Israelites were slaves in Egypt, but God provided a way for them to get out by sending Moses to negotiate with Pharaoh. When Pharaoh finally relented and released them, the Israelites followed God's leader, Moses, and God's leading, a pillar of cloud by day and a fire by night, as He led them to the Promised Land.

When the Israelites left Egypt, they weren't truly free yet. Sure, they were walking away from excessive oppression and mistreatment, but they knew Pharaoh was prone to changing his mind; so the Israelites were always looking over their shoulder to see if they were being pursued. Along their journey, they encountered the Red Sea. The Red Sea is so wide and so deep that there was no way 2.5 million Israelites would have been able to cross it on foot. And since there was no way 2.5 million Israelites would have been able to cross it on foot—and since they had just escaped from slavery in Egypt—they weren't exactly loaded with yachts and speedboats to help their predicament.

Actually, if you look at a map of the path that God led the Israelites on from Egypt to the Promised Land, you'd see that there was no logical reason for them to encounter the Red Sea in the first place. No modern-day GPS system would've taken them via the Red Sea, but God's wisdom is greater than man-made technology. He could see the value of the Israelites reaching that dead end before they could experience true freedom.

Once they reached the Red Sea, the sounds of approaching chariots made it clear that Pharaoh had indeed changed his mind; his army was on its way to bring the Israelites back to Egypt. So not only were they facing an impossible-to-cross obstacle in front of them, but their enemies were closing in behind them.

At that point the Israelites had to acknowledge and accept the fact that God was the only One who could get them across to freedom—they had to come to the end of their self-trust. And the moment God saw that they had stopped trusting in their own strength and started trusting Him to deliver them, God intervened. He came in and demonstrated His power by parting the Red Sea. He provided a dry, clear, ten-mile path for the Israelites to walk across. Walls of water thousands of feet high towered threateningly on both sides, but the Israelites, all 2.5 million of them, made it across with no problems. Once they were safely on the other side, water started crashing down on Pharaoh's army of approximately twenty thousand chariots who had closed the gap and were close on their heels. The Israelites found themselves once again looking over their shoulders, but this time it was to watch the defeat of their enemies by their God.

> They had to come to the end of their self-trust.

The Red Sea not only represented the end of their self-trust, it represented the beginning of their freedom. No longer did they have to fear their enemies catching them again. From that point on, they could focus on the relationship God was providing as He led them to the Promised Land.

The Promised Land was a real place, but it is also an analogy depicting the freedom that God wants for all of His children. It is a picture of the true relationship God offers—a life of joy, hope, and provision. In order to reach the Promised Land, and before anyone can enter a relationship with God, they must come to the end of their self-trust and acknowledge that God's path is the only way to heaven. It truly is the only way. But if we hold on to the belief that we can somehow earn our way into heaven, we'll find that our paths will take us in circles to nowhere. Eventually, we must all hit the dead end of self-trust.

The Law

If you know anything about church history or have spent time studying the Bible, you know that the Old Testament (the first major portion of the Bible) is full of laws and rules (e.g., dietary laws, how you can wear your hair and earrings, etc.).

Try this. Sit down and read Leviticus. You'll find yourself thinking of every unbearable circumstance—the dentist, cleaning toilets, folding laundry, or even watching a chick flick [okay, so those are mine!]—that would still be better than persevering through a single chapter. Leviticus is filled with rules and guidelines. It's as if all the angels up in heaven were joking around as God was writing the law, and they were all trying to throw in their two cents:

"Hey, tell them they can't do this."

"Oh, and throw this rule in too; let's just see what they say to that."

That's how frustrating trying to follow every point of the law is, but that's not why God wrote the law. We don't have to try and live our lives according to all of those rules: "For you no longer live under the requirements of the law. Instead, you live under the freedom of God's grace" (Rom. 6:14).

After Jesus came to the earth and the New Testament was written, the purpose of the law became evident. It never was about keeping all of the rules so a person could be in right relationship with God; the purpose of the law was to show the Israelites, and all who came after them, that they could not be good enough on their own strength: "God's law was given so that all people could see how sinful they were. But as people sinned more and more, God's wonderful grace became more abundant" (Rom. 5:20).

Those who tried to follow the law were flawed humans incapable of being perfect. The law merely showed them they had to come to the end of their self-trust. They could not have a true relationship with God until they put their entire trust in Him. The law was merely a tutor to illustrate one thing: no person can do it without God. "For no one can ever be made right with God by doing what the law commands. The law simply shows us how sinful we are" (Rom. 3:20).

Works

The idea of coming to the end of your self-trust stands in stark contrast to what society in general believes about faith in God. I have spent countless hours talking to people about Jesus, and while I enjoy it, I've noticed many become uncomfortable discussing their beliefs.

Here's a question I periodically ask, "If you're standing at the gates of heaven, and God asks you, 'Why should I let you into heaven?' what would you tell Him?" Often, when people answer this question, they tend to focus on the accomplishments they believe will earn them a place in heaven:

"Well, I've been a pretty good person, so God will let me in."

"I haven't done anything that bad, so I'm going to heaven."

"You know, I've done some really good things, so I deserve to go to heaven."

All of these answers are based on this idea that there's a cosmic scale at the pearly gates. As each person attempts to enter, all of their good deeds, little and big, are piled on one side of the scale. On the other side, all of their bad deeds are stacked. The basic presumption is that as long as the good deeds outweigh the bad, then that person deserves to go to heaven. Even if the scale only slightly favors the good deeds, they believe they're still going to be allowed into heaven with God. This line of thinking is based on what *I* must do to get to heaven or how many good works *I* must perform before God will accept me.

> Until we stop relying on ourselves to justify our place in heaven, we will not be following His way.

God needs us to come to the end of our self-trust because *I* has nothing to do with our relationship with God. God is the only way, and until we stop relying on ourselves to justify our place in heaven, we will not be following His way.

See for yourself what God says:

> But now God has shown us a way to be made right with him without keeping the requirements of the law, as was promised in the writings of Moses and the prophets long ago. We are made right with God by placing our faith in Jesus Christ. And this is true for everyone who believes, no matter who we are.
>
> For everyone has sinned; we all fall short of God's glorious standard. Yet God, with unde-served kindness, declares that we are righteous. He did this through Christ Jesus when he freed

us from the penalty for our sins. For God presented Jesus as the sacrifice for sin. People are made right with God when they believe that Jesus sacrificed his life, shedding his blood. This sacrifice shows that God was being fair when he held back and did not punish those who sinned in times past, for he was looking ahead and including them in what he would do in this present time. God did this to demonstrate his righteousness, for he himself is fair and just, and he declares sinners to be right in his sight when they believe in Jesus.

Can we boast, then, that we have done anything to be accepted by God? No, because our acquittal is not based on obeying the law. It is based on faith. (Rom. 3:21–27)

New Testament Rules

Okay, so we've seen the purpose of the Old Testament Law. That's freeing. Before we get too excited we need to realize that the New Testament isn't without its own list of dos and don'ts. Let's take a minute and think about the purpose for those. If God's design were for each person to strictly adhere to this list, would any of us qualify for heaven? Another way of looking at it is if Jesus really just required that our good deeds outweigh the bad, would yours honestly add up to be enough?

Let's take a look at the Scriptures and see exactly which good deeds we're to follow if we were to earn our own salvation.

Look at 1 Thessalonians 5:15, "Make sure that nobody pays back wrong for wrong" (NIV). Well, I'm only halfway through this verse, and I'm out already. Perhaps some of you are reading this and thinking you would never pay back evil for evil, so you still qualify.

Let's continue with the rest of the verse, "But always try to be kind to each other and to everyone else." Who's still in now? A few of you? Okay, verse 16, "Be joyful always." Most of you are out now.

Still think you qualify? Verse 17, "Pray continually." Another segment of you just fell off. Verse 18, "Give thanks in all circumstances." The rest of you are out. "Do not put out the Spirit's fire; do not treat prophecies with contempt. Test everything. Hold on to the good. Avoid every kind of evil" (vv. 19–22). How are you doing with that list? How is this path working out for you? This is just one passage, and there are many similar passages in the New Testament.

When I was a young Christian, I set down to summarize the New Testament law. I was going to read through the entire New Testament and write down all the dos and don'ts. I was kind of bummed there wasn't a Ten Commandments in the New Testament, so I decided I was going to make one for God. Plus, I wanted to have easy access to help me remember all of the things I was and wasn't supposed to do.

When I read 1 Peter 1:16, "Be holy," I thought, *This is not going to be a fruitful exercise.*

Why? Because I can't do that!

The list doesn't stop there. In Colossians 3, it tells us to forgive as Jesus forgave. First John 2:6 says that we should walk as Jesus walked.

Still thinking God expects us to do this on our own?

Matthew 5:11 and 44 tell us to be kind to people who hate us, and pray for them. Romans 8:37 says to consistently overcome. Ephesians 5:20 instructs us to give thanks in all situations. Philippians 4:6 says to never worry about anything but always have peace.

Never worry. Ever. Always be at peace. Are you still with me?

Philippians 4:4 tells us to rejoice in the Lord always. Philippians 2:15 says to stand out in bold contrast to the world. Matthew 16:24 says that we should hate ourselves and denounce our selfish desires. Colossians 3:1–2 instructs us to keep our focus on heavenly things.

We can't do it, right? But don't you see? That's the point. We have to come to the end of self-trust.

God Doesn't Grade on a Curve

I remember in high school learning a lesson. The teachers had a procedure set up to determine all of their students' grades by basing everything on a curve. So as a student, I didn't have to learn the material; I just had to outperform everyone in the class, which in some classes was easier than others.

In a particular class in high school, all I had to do was get a 69 percent. I knew everybody else in the class was going to do worse than that, so I would automatically be bumped to a 100 percent. This is a terrible system by which to determine if a student understands the material. But it served me well.

> There's this mentality that if I do just enough so that I'm not as bad as those other people, then surely God will let me into heaven.

The world, however, does not grade on a curve. Our bosses don't grade on a curve. Our spouses don't grade on a curve. Ironically, as Christians we expect God to grade on a curve. There's this mentality that if I do just enough so that I'm not as bad as those other people, then surely God will let me into heaven. But this is why God insists we put an end to our self-trust. We can never do enough. He is the only way.

Broken Isn't Always Bad

A word that typifies coming to the end of self-trust is *brokenness*. What is brokenness? Brokenness is giving up on your own confidence and ability to manage life. When God takes you to that place, you realize you can't do it all on your own. But you also find faith in the One who can.

Several years ago, my son, Ben, who was five years old at the time, traveled with me to Cleveland, Tennessee, to a youth camp where I was the speaker for the week. This particular camp was held in the beautiful hill country on the edge of the Great Smoky Mountains. It is truly a majestic spot in nature, offering everything from ropes courses to white-water rafting to wave pools to paintball.

One of the must-dos at the camp is a 1,000-foot zip line that follows the downhill slope of the mountain. This thing makes even the coolest of teenage guys scream like little girls. At the bottom of this mountain is a staging area where equipment is handed out and instructions are given. On the afternoon that Ben and I decided to do the zip line, an overzealous college student gave us way more information about zip lines than we ever needed to know, including details about a tragic, fatal accident that had occurred the previous year.

As we were getting our harnesses and helmets on, the attendant asked how much Ben weighed. I had no idea. So I guessed; 55 pounds? He said that it was okay because fifty is the smallest a kid can be. (When I got home, my wife, Meredith, informed me that he only weighed 42 pounds. So he was probably the smallest kid to ever ride on this 1,000-foot zip line.)

My son and I, both terrified, began the exhausting fifteen-minute hike up the hill. At the top of the hill, they clipped us in side-by-side. At this point it was evident Ben did not weigh 50 pounds. The staffer almost went down the line himself trying to hang on to Ben's waist and keep him from being pulled down the line by the weight of the cable.

"Are you ready?" he asked. My son and I nodded yes, and on the count of three, eyes the size of silver dollars, we stepped off the platform. My friends, watching at the bottom of the mountain, said that as Ben rode down the zip line, every muscle in his body was flexed hanging on to that line for dear life.

At the bottom, I asked Ben what he thought, and his response was, "It was long. My arms are really tired."

"Why are your arms tired?" I asked.

"Because if I would've let go, I would have fallen into the trees and died," he said.

Ben didn't realize he was clipped into the line, safe and secure. His safety had nothing to do with his ability or strength to hold on to the zip line. With all of his might, he hung desperately onto something that was actually holding on to him. Had he realized that one simple truth, he would have had a completely different ride—and his muscles wouldn't have cramped for three days.

Many Christians live with the same illusion that they are close to Jesus because they are holding onto Him with both hands. In other words, they believe their energy, effort, and strength keep them attached to the Savior after they are fastened in. But, in fact, they are harnessed in to God Almighty, and He's the One doing the great work in them.

The River Wild

That camp is in the Smoky Mountains along the Ocoee River. This river is so impressive that the rafting events in the '96 Summer Olympics were held there.

The instructors are blonde, cut out of stone, abs that are so defined they don't have a six-pack, they have a twelve-pack, each wearing daisy-duke shorts. These freaks of nature explained what kind of rapids we were going to encounter, including a class four called Hell's Hole, which thrilled the teens. The guides were even inclined to lower their voices when they said "Hell's Hole" so you actually believed demons circle it.

At this point, the instructors became very serious and explained that the number-one goal is to not fall out of the raft. Hmm, really? But if you do, relax, put your feet up, put your booty down, pull your knees into your chest, and face the way you're traveling. Therefore, if you're headed to a tree or stump or boulder, you can kick off instead of getting tangled up in it. The cardinal rule emphasized by all of the instructors was to never ever, ever, ever try standing in the water. Ever. If one rock or crevice catches your foot, it will snap your ankle or leg. Or it can pin you underwater so that you can't get another breath, and you drown. *Sign me up!*

After my raft made it down the river, we went straight to the spot we knew teens were going to want to watch—Hell's Hole. That makes great video footage for the camp share service.

When we got to the area near Hell's Hole, we encountered the "lifeguard." It's not really fair to call him a lifeguard because he was more like *Baywatch* meets *Dukes of Hazzard*. He had cutoffs on and this rope hanging around his thick, chiseled chest with an orange buoy hanging from his shoulder. In front of him was a line strung across the river, tied near the lifeguard on the other side.

We posted ourselves close to him and began watching the rafts fly by. Kids were screaming and crying. All of a sudden a girl fell out of her raft. We heard her scream, and the girl went right under the water. Almost a minute later, hundreds of yards down the river, she bobbed to the surface still screaming. Both guards just sat there eating their deviled-egg-and-ham sandwiches. They didn't jump to her rescue. They didn't even flinch.

A few minutes later, a boy flew out of his raft. Hundreds of yards down the river he popped back up again screaming. Again, the lifeguards did not move.

Then, along came another raft. A woman flew out of the boat and screamed, "Helllllppppp m—" as she was dragged underwater. What happened over the next eight seconds was one of the coolest things I had ever seen. One lifeguard took this flotation device off of his shoulder and hurled it at least forty feet across the river. The other guard grabbed it in midair and hooked it to a line. Then he slid down into the water like Indiana Jones. It was like a rodeo guy getting a calf because within seconds they had the woman out of the water and up on the bank.

I looked at the video guy and eagerly asked, "Did you get that?" Stunned, he shook his head, mouth wide open, camera pointing to the ground. I looked up at the lifeguard and said, "You have got to do that again! We missed it. You have to do it again." He assured us there would be another chance.

More kids screamed, went under, then popped back up farther down the river. No movement. Finally, another kid fell out of the boat screaming, "Help m—" and under the water he went. Just like before, the guards sprang into action. This time, we got it all on video.

The End of Self-Trust

When one of the lifeguards went on break, I told him, "You have to explain this to me. You watched dozens of people fall out of their boats, and you didn't move, but there were two or three today that you guys did the coolest thing I've ever seen saving these people and getting them out of the water in just a matter of seconds. Why those people?"

His answer was simple yet profound. "Here's our philosophy: people pay to ride this ride. So, when we hear screaming, we assume they're enjoying it. You don't take people off of a roller coaster when you hear them screaming. But there are a couple of words that move us into action. Those two words are 'help me.'"

That's the end of self-trust. When we get to a place where we realize we can't do it on our own, yet we have faith in the One who can, we declare with all our passion, "Help me." Those two words are like platinum. At that moment, God jumps in and shows us He's already taken care of everything.

> When we get to a place where we realize we can't do it on our own, yet we have faith in the One who can, we declare with all our passion, "Help me."

In Him

Like I said before, I truly believe the God of the Bible is a good God. He wants a relationship with each of us, and He's done everything in His power to make it possible to know Him.

Look again at 1 Thessalonians 5. At the end of the list of dos and don'ts, verse 23 says, "May God himself, the God of peace, sanctify you through and through.

May your whole spirit, soul and body be kept blameless at the coming of our Lord Jesus Christ" (NIV).

Did you catch the shift?

He starts with all those things that we're supposed to do—never get angry, return evil with joy, always pray, etc. But then he changes gears and says may the God of peace keep you holy. Who sanctifies you? God does. He's the One making us blameless in every way. You don't earn blamelessness. Verse 24 continues, "The one who calls you is faithful and *he will do it*" (emphasis mine).

God's doing it. Not you. Not me. Just God. See how good He is?

If you've had a relationship with God and believed that God was your copilot as you navigated through life, then I'm here to tell you, He wasn't even on the plane. God's not anybody's copilot. He not only wants to be the pilot; He wants to be the copilot, runway, airplane, air, destination, everything. He wants to be life itself. Acts 17:28 says, "In him we live and move and have our being" (NIV). All of life—in Him. But we can only truly experience that when we give it all up to Him.

Every person, before entering into a true relationship with God and getting on His path to heaven, must come to a point of brokenness and cry out, "God, help me." That's all God requires.

And the result of God's gracious gift is very different from the result of that one man's sin. For Adam's sin led to condemnation, but God's free gift leads to our being made right with God, even though we are guilty of many sins. (Rom. 5:16)

What Now?

Maybe you're ready to cry to God for help right now. Maybe not. It's a decision that should not be taken lightly. Some of you may need some more time to process, but others of you may be ready to make that decision right now.

If you have never come to the end of your self-trust before now, but want to commit to God, then I would consider it a privilege to help you receive the free gift of salvation. If you're not ready, no problem. Earmark this page, and when you're ready, come back to it.

For those of you who are ready to believe that God's way is the only way to heaven, and you want to stop trusting in your own ability to get to heaven, then take a moment to pray your own "Help me!" prayer to God.

If the words don't come naturally, feel free to pray something like this . . .

Dear Jesus,

I know I am a sinner, and I have trusted myself instead of trusting You. I've messed things up, but right now I ask You to come into my life as my Lord. I want You to call the shots in my life now. I want You to be my Savior, my Forgiver, and my Best Friend. In the best way I know how, I am turning my life over to You and asking You to help me. I turn my back on my sin and my self-trust.

I receive Jesus and the gift of salvation.

Thank You, Jesus, for saving me.

Amen.

If you meant it with all of your heart, then the Bible indicates that Jesus is now your Lord and Savior. You are on the path of ultimate grace that God has forged for you. This is the best decision you have ever made. Congratulations!

Study Questions

1. Describe a dead end that you've personally encountered. How did you respond?

2. List some of the New Testament dos and don'ts you have tried to follow to make a way to God.

3. What is the purpose of "rules" listed in the Old and New Testament?

4. If you prayed your "Help me!" prayer to God for the first time or renewed your commitment to God, then take a moment and write down today's date and exactly what you chose to do.

Chapter Four

Religion Is So That . . .

I most especially call myself a deist/theist because at my grandmother's funeral a pair of "god-fearing" Christians that happened to be outside the Catholic church where we were having her services were "kind enough and concerned enough" for the state of our mortal souls that they condemned my entire family to hell for being Catholics and Jews. Thanks, Christianity . . . much appreciated. They're both lucky I remembered the teachings of Christ that day, and they're lucky my Jewish relatives didn't hear them because they'd have been arrested if I hadn't dealt with the situation myself and kept them away from the family.

—B. S. [Excerpted from www.jesushates religion.com message board]

A friend of mine recently surrendered his life to God. At the time he prayed the "Help me!" prayer, he had a wife and two girlfriends. Obviously, he knew that if being accepted by God had anything to do with stacking up enough good works, he was out. Hitting the dead end of self-trust was paramount for him. He knew he couldn't argue he was perfect or holy. He knew he couldn't trust himself. He needed a Savior.

But, unfortunately, just praying the "salvation" prayer doesn't guarantee him a smooth journey from salvation to heaven. What I cautioned him (and I'm cautioning you) to be aware of is the dead end that many, possibly all, Christians hit *during* their journey.

When a person surrenders all to God and prays that "salvation" prayer, it doesn't mean the temptation to trust in good works disappears. No matter what point you're on in your journey, the performance path—the path where you earn your acceptance and favor with God—is always a tempting detour. It's a path that requires you to veer away from God's path. It's a path that looks right. It's a path that looks holy. It's a path that looks like something God would have created. But it isn't.

God created only one path to Him. At no point in your journey does God's path evolve into a performance path. Be aware. Performance is a trap. God never changes lanes. It's never about your religion. It's always the same grace path.

Whether it is ego, pride, or ignorance, many people recognize they are initially accepted by God based on His grace. But then they buy into the belief that the time between salvation and heaven is all about what they do for God. They pray. They read the Bible. They share Jesus with others. They. They. They.

> God never changes lanes. It's never about your religion. It's always the same grace path.

When people veer onto the performance path, then they will have to hit another dead end—the end of religion—before they can steer back onto God's perfect path. God will see to it that believers eventually hit this dead end because God knows when good works become a requirement for His grace, it's no longer real grace:

> It is the same today, for a few of the people of Israel have remained faithful because of God's grace—his undeserved kindness in choosing them. And since it is through God's kindness, then it is not by their good works. For

in that case, God's grace would not be what it really is—free and undeserved. (Rom. 11:5–6)

Gotta Have Faith

Granted, as a pastor I do teach that reading your Bible, praying, sharing Jesus, etc., are all good things. But here's the difference: God never bases His acceptance of us on our performance of or completion of these tasks. Religion, on the other hand, is founded upon performance. Hebrews 11 tells us that the only thing that impresses God is our faith in Him; whereas, the essence of religion is man's attempt to somehow convince himself that he can jump through enough performance hoops in order for God to give him the approving nod. In a way, these acts of self-righteousness are people's attempts to validate themselves before God, but in reality they are separating themselves from God.

In the New Testament, there's a story about two brothers. The older brother obeyed his father and remained faithful to work for him and take care of him. The younger brother decided to cash in on his inheritance before the father was even dead. Then he went and squandered the entire sum on partying and selfish behavior. In the end, the younger brother ran out of money, realized the error of his ways, and came back to find himself welcomed with opened arms by his father. When his father chose to throw a huge party in celebration of the boy returning, the older brother was indignant. He refused to attend the party.

Isn't it ironic that the righteousness of the older brother made him equally distant from the father as the unrighteousness of the younger brother? Yet, Jesus ended the story with the younger brother restoring his relationship with the father while the older brother refuses to join the wel-come-home party and puts distance between himself and his father.

> Our acts of self-righteousness can actually be more damaging and unfruitful than acts of unrighteousness.

Jesus' message is clear. Our acts of self-righteousness can actually be more damaging and unfruitful than acts of unrighteousness. Why? Because the unrighteous man knows he needs help; but the self-righteous man doesn't acknowledge that he needs help.

Relentless Reminders

Before we can even get on the right path to God, we must acknowledge that God's way is the only way.

The first dead end—self-trust—is a place we must hit before our personal relationship with God begins. There is nothing we can do to earn it.

Once we're on that path of grace, we must relentlessly remind ourselves until we get to heaven that there is nothing we can do that will cause us to earn our salvation. It's when we veer off the path of grace and try to use good deeds to earn our salvation that God purposefully directs us—to the dead end of religion.

It's *Because* Not *So That*

The difference between the right and wrong motive for doing good deeds is *so that* versus *because*. If you're doing good deeds such as praying, going to church, studying the Bible, *so that* God will accept you or give you a gold star, then you've made your journey with Christ about yourself. You have taken God out of the equation. Religion is *so that*. People who live by *so that* are miserable.

But when you do all of these good things *because* Jesus saved you, *because* He is your Savior, and *because* He lives inside of you, then you will effectively steer clear of the performance path.

My friend Tom learned this the hard way. For Tom, it was less of a performance path and more of a race car speedway with dangerous curves, wipeouts, and the never-ending frustration of trying to finish on top by winning the approval of God. Growing up, his life, both spiritual and physical, was all about the performance. Whether it was school, sports, or religion, he was always striving to win approval.

> If you're doing good deeds such as praying, going to church, studying the Bible, *so that* God will accept you or give you a gold star, then you've made your journey with Christ about yourself.

Tom's parents followed generations of Irish Catholic tradition of following the faith but never questioning it. He learned from an early age that religion was a ritual to follow based on the time of year or stage of life he was experiencing—baptism at birth, first communion, altar boy, first confession, confirmation, marriage, and then repeat with his wife and kids. What was always lacking was a relationship based on love. Despite living a lifestyle in order to please God, he never felt truly loved until January 3, 2002, when he prayed according to the Bible for God to save him.

Everything changed after that. Tom no longer was afraid of God. He no longer tried to impress God with his good deeds—his favorite was helping a turtle across the road; surely God was impressed with that one, right? He stopped trying to impress God and accepted the fact that God loved him unconditionally. Tom was also freed from his addictions, and he experienced a peace in his life that had never been there before. Tom knew that God loved him no matter how many Hail Marys he said.

Everything went well for a while, but soon the performance path lured Tom back. In Tom's words:

> The Lord blessed me with a level of fulfillment in life I never would have dreamed possible, including helping me as my wife battled brain cancer, and all the different things each of us deals with in life while raising children. My business was thriving and my wife was cancer free by the grace of our Holy Father. Even with my faith growing, I fell back into performance when the Devil found a way back into my life.
>
> In 2009, the recession hit my business hard—I thought it was me. I did not give enough, but I did not have the money to give. I did not have enough faith. He had given me so much, but I did not please Him. After coming to grips with the fact I can do nothing for the Creator of the universe—He does all for me, so all I need is to

trust and have faith—I came out of a hell I never want to experience again.

Today I am living how the Word teaches me—I only can perform because Christ is in me. There is nothing I can do alone without His Spirit flowing through every aspect of my life.

Just like Tom, it's vital we remain on the path of grace. It's a pure lifestyle. When purity is our life, then God is free to do great works in and through us.

Beware of Mixing Business with Grace

Do you ever wonder why some high-and-mighty, pious spiritual leaders seem to "all of a sudden" fall into wicked and sinful lifestyles? Often they are living by religion. Even though their ministries are accomplishing wonderful things, they themselves are miserable. Many jump ship and dive into the world of unrighteousness, out of frustration of never feeling good enough.

When people choose to follow a religion, their primary motive is to crack the code on God *so that* they can get God to bless them. God is love. And while it's possible for us to obey and not love, it's impossible for us to truly love and not obey. The love comes first. When we get those two out of order, we begin a journey God did not design for us. We will be miserable.

In the business world, everything is centered on production. If one achieves the desired results, a reward is imminent. But that's not true in the spiritual world. Christianity is not built around performance; it's built around the person of Jesus Christ.

This concept is not only something people who do not follow God need to understand, but Christians also need to understand it. Many Christians are struggling to make their lives count for God only to find out life isn't working like they thought it would. While they are sincere in their commitment and have given their best effort, they are frustrated because they can't achieve what they think they should be able to achieve. When a Christian is focused on works, at some point, he/she begins to wonder, "Is this all there is? Is this all Jesus died for?" And if they resign themselves to that numbness, they will quit and walk away from God.

> When people choose to follow a religion, their primary motive is to crack the code on God *so that* they can get God to bless them.

In turn, those who don't believe in God see Christians living a life of frustration and disappointment, and it tarnishes their view of God. Honestly, who would want to follow a God that requires so much work with so little reward?

I know all Christians desire to be successful when it comes to the things of God, but it doesn't mean they have to buy into the lie that success comes only through hard work. Success in the Christian life comes from God's grace, which He has made available to all who believe.

> Christianity is not built around performance; it's built around the person of Jesus Christ.

The Christians who understand and live out this truth exemplify a biblical perspective of God. Those Christians persuade others that it's good to follow God's way. They not only experience a blessed and full life, but they stir within others a desire to live a similar life.

When we mix business with grace, our focus shifts from God's way to finding ways to prove ourselves through hard work. Success in the business world comes through hard work, but we must abandon that model when it comes to the spiritual. It's all about Jesus Christ.

The Jordan River

Remember the children of Israel we discussed in the last chapter? After God miraculously made a way for them to cross the Red Sea, and after they put an end to their self-trust, they still dealt with the temptation to rely on their own strength and wisdom to get them to the Promised Land. When God saw they were relying more on themselves and less on Him, He drove them into the second dead end of their journey—the Jordan River. (The story begins in Joshua 3 if you want to read it for yourself.)

The majority of people who've actually seen the Jordan River more than likely saw it during a time when it was calm and looked more like a creek than a raging rapid. But when the children of Israel reached the Jordan, it was harvest time. The Sea of Galilee, 700 feet below sea level, flows through the Jordan for about seventy miles until it empties into the Dead Sea, 1,300 feet below sea level, giving the Jordan its name. Jordan means "descender." During harvest time, the Jordan swells to rafting-level-five proportions and creates twenty-seven major rapids. Can you imagine rafting over that? I've always wanted to take teenagers during harvest time to raft the Jordan River. I keep thinking if this preaching thing doesn't work out, I'll go ahead and start a business leading rafting trips on the Jordan. I'll call it "Alex's Arab Adventures."

Back to the story, the Hebrews have hit yet another dead end and now find themselves camped for three days on the banks of the river. As the rapids are swirling and hissing, the river is preaching a four-word sermon to the people: You can't do it.

Mission Impossible

One summer, I spoke at a youth camp for a group of churches. The camp was held at a resort in Gulf Shores, Alabama. Because the location was a fun one, Meredith and the kids decided to come along with me. At one point in the journey, I asked Meredith to drive. (Keep in mind, in the years and years that we have been married, including when we dated, Meredith has probably driven the car with me in it a total of fewer than ten hours—she does not drive fast enough for my impatience.)

Back when personal navigation units first came out, I had purchased a TomTom. This was our first time using a GPS system. Unfortunately, while Meredith was driving, the GPS came unplugged and eventually died. I was reading in the passenger seat, assuming the GPS would tell us where to go. When I realized we were lost, Meredith had driven over an hour out of the way. I did not respond well.

At that point, we had a decision to make: turn around or look for an alternate way to get back on track. I grabbed a map. Between the map and the GPS, we found a bridge and made our way toward it.

As we got closer, the GPS began indicating that we had twelve miles but almost two hours left to go. Then, it stated we had six miles and one hour left. I was sure the GPS was wrong until we pulled into a line of traffic in the middle of many orange cones. With cars lined up both in front of us and behind, I finally saw a sign that said, "Ferry Entrance."

This sparked a fun conversation between Meredith and me, so I tried to diffuse the tension by saying, "Look, kids! A sno-cone stand." We all got out and headed toward the stand. As the lady was making our sno-cones, I asked her when the ferry was coming, how long it took to cross the water, etc.

I got out my wallet to pay the lady, and I realized I had no cash and the ferry wouldn't take credit cards. Now my conversation with Meredith reached a new level of fun as we discussed what kind of father takes his family on a trip with no cash.

As we walked back to the car, a random lady asked, "Are you Alex Himaya?" I said yes with a puzzled look on my face. She told me she was from Arkansas, and the previous year I had preached at her teenager's youth camp where he had surrendered his life to Jesus.

I said, "Praise the Lord. I need twenty dollars."

She asked, "What?" and I told her our story.

She immediately got twenty dollars from her husband, and I looked at Meredith and said, "See, I told you it would all work out."

Meredith responded, "Are you kidding me? This could only happen to you."

Here's the point. We ended up on that ferry because our GPS led us this way. Similarly, the Israelites ended up at the banks of the Jordan River because their GPS, God, took them that way. Crossing the Jordan was not the easiest, nor the most direct, route for the Hebrews to take, but God's GPS navigates His followers into the land of grace and freedom with no regard for how crazy the route may appear.

Remember, grace is something that cannot be earned. It's a gift. God designs situations to bring believers to the end of their religion. Likewise, He'll steer us into situations with the purpose of putting an end to our religion. No matter how hard we try, we can never live a victorious Christian life on our own. It's impossible. Our job is to abide.

Joshua, who replaced Moses as the leader of the Israelites, got it. He trusted God. He knew God was bringing the children of Israel to the dead end of their religion to show them that He alone is their bridge over troubled waters. They had to be reminded that they could not do it alone. God was their only bridge. The children of Israel were not capable of saving themselves.

> God was their only bridge. The children of Israel were not capable of saving themselves.

Keep in mind that the Bible calls the Hebrews God's *chosen* people. Another interesting note about the children of Israel—God chose them before He led them into the wilderness and gave them the law at Mt. Sinai. Think about the theology of that—they were already chosen, and then God gave them the law. Don't you see? The law never had anything to do with being chosen by God. It was a tutor to teach them they couldn't do it on their own.

So for forty years, they wandered through the wilderness, practiced the rules, and lived by religion. But they never got to the Promised Land on their own effort. And when they reached the river Jordan, it stood as a physical illustration that they couldn't do it on their own. They had to put an end to their religion.

Poison

Religion is poison because it kills every opportunity you will ever have to experience genuine intimacy with God. The underlying foundation of religion is performance, but God is not impressed by our performances. The only thing that impresses God is faith—faith that He alone is the way to heaven (Heb. 11:6). The person who's trying to achieve spiritual success by religious performance may think he's making good time, but he's driving in circles. The essence of religion is man's attempt to somehow convince himself he's jumped through enough hoops for God to give him the approving nod, but our acts of self-righteousness actually separate us from God.

Have you ever seen the trick where a performer can keep twelve plates spinning on top of twelve different sticks? Throughout the performance, the man runs up and down the row fascinating us with his ability to keep all twelve going. This looks a lot like religion: the plates are what we value—the aspects of religion that we believe need to be in the air and stay spinning. But inevitably, the performer will tire from running back and forth and trying to keep all of those plates spinning. In fact, I think that sometimes God comes and knocks the plates off and lets them break even before the performer falters.

This performance puts distance between people and God, but God sent Jesus to remove that distance. God said that He came to give life—a rich and satisfying life—not to give us a life bound to a list of rituals and ethics (John 10:10).

God Never Goes Too Far

If you've always believed God will never let you face something that you can't handle, you've been horribly mislead. In the following verse, the author, Paul, is addressing *temptation*—God never tempts us. It's like the apple in the Garden of Eden—ever been tempted by an apple? God knew better than that—if He was going to tempt you, He would've put caramel on it. The Devil is always the tempter.

> The temptations in your life are no different from what others experience. And God is faithful. He will not allow the temptation to be more than you can stand. When you are tempted, he will show you a way out so that you can endure. (1 Cor. 10:13)

Look at the verse again in a different version:

> No temptation has seized you except what is common to man. And God is faithful; he

will not let you be tempted beyond what you can bear. But when you are tempted, he will also provide a way out so that you can stand up under it. (1 Cor. 10:13 NIV)

God says that He will never allow you to be *tempted* beyond what you can handle; He always gives you a way out. It doesn't mean He won't put you in situations that you can't handle. If that were true, I'd be in big trouble because He does it to me all the time.

In 2 Corinthians 1:8–9, Paul is talking about the troubles he faced in his life. If you don't know anything about Paul, he was a man who at one point persecuted and killed Christians; but after he encountered God, he dedicated his life to teaching others about His grace and forgiveness. From the point of his conversion, he shared his testimony and taught thousands of people about God. He's also the author of most of the books in the New Testament. So when you read that Paul— this great man of God—had troubles, you know it's not something exclusively for non-Christians. But as it turned out, Paul's troubles were the best things that could have ever happened. Instead of Paul trusting in his own strength or wisdom to get out of it, Paul was forced to trust God totally:

We don't want you in the dark, friends, about how hard it was when all this came down on us in Asia province. It was so bad we didn't think we were going to make it. We felt like we'd been sent to death row, that it was all over for us. As it turned out, it was the best thing that could have happened. Instead of trusting in our own strength or wits to get out of it, we were forced to trust God totally—not a bad idea since he's the God who raises the dead! And he did it, rescued us from certain doom. And he'll do it again, rescuing us as many times as we need rescuing. (2 Cor. 1:8–10 *The Message*)

God allowed Paul and his team to face situations that would cause them to come to the end of their religion. Even while he was there, God never left Paul. God rescued Paul from certain doom, and He'll rescue you too. Everyone needs rescuing at one time or another. God will even allow us to get into situations we feel we cannot handle, and when we finally accept the dead end of religion, He will come and rescue us.

Doesn't it feel as though we sometimes face problems that seem to come out of left field—problems that are excessive or beyond our strength to handle? Paul reached a point where he admitted he began to despair his own life. He even said he felt like he was on death row. Ever felt like that? Remember Paul's lesson: "This happened that we might not rely on ourselves but on God, who raises the dead." There is hope.

Only One

Only one person can live the Christian life. You're not the one—it is Jesus. He's the only one who can live the Christian life. He will live it through us and in us when we give up on our own religion and learn to abide in Him.

The invitation to the Promised Land shows us how persistent God is in bringing about the good He has promised to those who belong to Him. He's not going to quit on you. There is nothing you can ever do to cause God to shrug His shoulders and walk away from you. He's always present and He

> There is nothing you can ever do to cause God to shrug His shoulders and walk away from you.

wants to bring you to a place where He can do for you everything He has planned.

The Israelites lived in the wilderness, relying on their own religion, for forty years. Some of you have lived there longer. Religious behavior is your way to control your lives and to control God, yet the only way to freedom is total abandonment to God.

Surrender to Him. Take a leap of faith. While it may seem scary, it's only scary to the extent that you don't know the character of God. When you know the character of God, it's not scary to leap into His arms.

Study Questions

1. What are the consequences of choosing the performance path over the path of God's grace?

2. Name three examples of rules and rituals Christ followers can get caught up in doing while trying to earn God's approval.

3. What are ways you can stay accountable so that you don't veer off God's path of grace? Who could help you with this?

4. When was a time when you felt God walk away from you or you walked away from God? How was your relationship restored?

Chapter Five

From Works to Grace

Religion is worthless. It got me nowhere. I grew up in a legalistic church and home, and I had a pastor for a grandfather. I sat in a room of people who did nothing but teach the philosophy of the do not: do not drink, do not curse, do not have sex, don't dance in church, keep your hands down during worship, and wear your best for Jesus. Of all of the things I hated about my upbringing, I think I hated the pretense the most. Why waste your time trying to look like something you aren't? Why can't people be real and up-front? Don't people need to show their hearts instead of their Sunday best? Would outsiders not feel more comfortable in a real church instead of a fake one? It's hard to believe in grace and mercy and redemption when the very people who have access to those things would prefer to stand with their own arms crossed and their eyebrows lowered, and judge my lack of perfection. I'd rather spend my time with people who are honest about their screw-ups than to waste five hours on Sunday with people who truly don't care about the person sitting next to them. I'm tired of pretending, but more so, I'm tired of feeling like I will have to.

I did post this under a false name. Why? Because I probably sit next to you on Sunday mornings, and I'm just as self-conscious as the rest of the world. How do I know I won't be ushered out the back door for having radical thoughts on a forgotten gospel? How can I trust people who say one thing on Sunday and something completely different on Monday morning?

—Anonymous [Excerpted from www.jesus hatesreligion.com message board]

Have you ever sung the lyrics to a song . . . incorrectly? You thought you were singing it correctly, but then later you found out that you'd been singing it wrong for years. There's actually a term for that—*mondegreen*—you can look that up.

Anyway, I remember the song "Raspberry Beret"[3] by Prince. I always sang, "She wore a raspberry parade, the kind you buy at a secondhand store," which makes no sense. How do you buy a parade at a secondhand store?

I used to butcher Michael Jackson's songs too. When I sang Jackson's "Billie Jean," I used to sing, "But the Chad is not my son." The Chad? Who's "the Chad"? And what does he have to do with this song? The correct lyrics are "But the kid is not my son," which makes a lot more sense.[4]

Have you ever watched a crime scene show on TV? The detectives will talk with eyewitnesses, but they also recognize that eyewitness accounts are highly unreliable. Because of this, most detectives make their decisions based on the evidence—the hard facts. What's interesting is that eyewitnesses will swear that they remember what really happened, but the detectives know that talking to multiple witnesses at the same crime scene will always result in vastly different accounts of the same event. For example, some remember the suspect having facial hair; others swear he is clean-shaven; some remember him wearing a hat; others promise they saw his shaggy hair.

Memory's a funny thing. We think we remember things exactly as they happened, but research has shown that more often than not, our memory is far from perfect. Whether it's remembering lyrics to a song or teachings about the Bible, it's very possible memory can change "the facts" in our minds.

Consider this, given the flaws of human memory, is it possible that some of the things we've been taught about the Bible weren't actually taught to us at all? We just remember it that way? And, even more likely, could it be that other people are teaching concepts from the Bible that they think they remember being taught to them? All of this is possible, and it could be skewing your perception of God—perceptions that the Bible doesn't even substantiate. For instance, most of us have heard that "God helps those who help themselves." This is often credited to the Bible, but, in reality, this was a proverb from Ben Franklin's *Poor Richard's Almanack*.

Many of you could be basing your assumptions about God on "facts" that you wouldn't be able to find in the Bible. You've assumed all of your life that you're right, but maybe you've been living by a song sheet that's not even correct or doesn't even exist. Could it be that in your religious walk there are things that you're buying into that just aren't true?

It's not so much what we don't know, but it's what we *think* we know that obstructs our vision and messes us up on the journey. For example, how many hours in your lifetime have you spent in the car lost because you *thought* you knew where you were going? Or as a child, how many hours of swim time did you miss because you ate just before you were going to get in the pool? I don't know about you, but as a kid, I used to try to starve myself so I wouldn't miss a moment of swim time.

You can only imagine my disappointment when I was older and found out that eating before swimming won't necessarily cause cramping. In fact, now experts believe that *not* eating before you swim causes cramps. All of those precious thirty-minute intervals I wasted sitting next to the pool, longing to jump in the cool water but knowing that if I did swim, I'd get cramps, drown, and die. All that time—hours, days, maybe even weeks of my childhood—wasted away.

The point is, we thought we knew what we were talking about when we kept kids out of the pool after eating. We thought we were right. Could this also be true in our perceptions of God? Maybe there are beliefs we hold dear and think we're right about, but the Bible doesn't support them.

For example, many people believe the will of God is a list of difficult things that God wants us to do and not do. But I'm telling you today—that's not the message of the Bible. As we come to know God, our focus needs to move away from the dos and the don'ts. When we focus on our works, we're more apt to get off course. Instead, the focus needs to be on Truth.

Burn Notice

So many people have been burned by church because they got tired of always doing, doing, doing (or not doing), yet they still felt empty inside—and even more tired than they were before. Actually, what I've found as I've hung out with and talked with people in my community, is that most of them have no trouble with God and, really, no beef with Jesus. It's the religion, rules, and unrealistic standards they were judged by that have shaped their views of God.

In the previous chapters of this book, I laid the foundation for where we're going. We began this journey by discussing how God, not the Devil, will see to it that you hit two dead ends: the end of self-trust and the end of religion. When you hit the end of self-trust, you come head-on into a collision with your self-confidence. You realize you can't do it alone: you need a Savior—Jesus Christ.

The second dead end that God directs believers to hit is essentially the dead end of religion—a place where people can't move any further because of the rules. A place where they no longer have to follow the dos and don'ts that they were convinced would get them into heaven and keep them out of hell. Those rules, quite honestly, are not going to usher anyone into a place of intimacy where God wants His children to dwell with Him. The only way to be intimate with God is to acknowledge that there is nothing you can do to earn your salvation. God has already done it all.

Honor Roll

I spent a lot of years going to school. I earned a bachelor's degree, a master's degree, and then a doctorate degree.

In these classes on the first day, each professor would give me a syllabus. In fact, many of my professors, in my master's degree especially, would essentially use the syllabus like a contract. It would include something along the lines of the following:

- If you want an A, here are the things you will do—you will write these papers, you will read these books, and you will perform this well on *a*, *b*, and *c* examinations.
- If you want a B, here are the things you can do . . .
- If you want a C, you can miss 50 percent of the class . . .

I could just decide up front which grade I wanted since I knew what the terms were.

Many Christians think this is the way God approaches them. They believe they have a list of choices about what kind of relationship they want with God. At the bottom rung of this contract, they could choose: "I don't want to have anything to do with God."

One notch above that is "I just want to get into heaven by the skin of my teeth," so their contract includes clauses that allow them to live like a sinner but still obtain all heaven has to offer.

Another notch up from that is "I want to be part of a church, but I don't want to do anything." Their contract allows them to take their place each Sunday but doesn't require them to actually do or follow anything God asks of them.

Moving up, they could choose, "I want to be a leader in my church." And at the top of the choices, "I want to be a minister." Basically these contracts would convince anyone that Billy Graham CLEP-ed the whole thing.

All of these contracts have one problem in common: they're written by people, not by God.

I think God really does have a contract with His believers, but it goes more like this: *You get an A. You get an A in My course because you are My child. And because I have saved you and entered into your life, and because you*

> I think God really does have a contract with His believers, but it goes more like this: *You get an A.*

*are an A student, I want you to act like it. I want you to
live like it. I want what's on the inside of you to come out
in the way you do life.*

Taste the Difference

Taste and see that the LORD is good. (Ps.
34:8)

Here the Bible uses the word *taste*: it could have
been any other word, but God chose a word that deals
with our experiences. He doesn't tell us to hear about
or read about God's goodness; He tells us to *taste* it.

It's like the difference between baby food and real
food. Remember when your kids ate baby food? My
kids are older now, but they all went through a stage
of eating jarred baby food. Many times I just wanted to
rush that process because I thought jarred baby food
was nasty. One of the meals that three of my kids loved
was spinach lasagna. Yuck! It had a horrible smell, and
when you opened it up, it looked like throw-up. Plus, it
was this organic brand, so you could buy a whole pizza
for the price of what was in just one of those tiny jars.
But my kids loved it.

Well, they loved it until they tasted the real thing. Once my kids experienced real food, they were determined to never go back to that jarred junk.

I remember when my brother's boys were just a year old, and I gave them ice cream. My brother was like, "Don't give them ice cream," but I did. And they loved it. We only see each other once a year for a week or so, but the one thing they remember about Uncle Alex is that he gave them ice cream. I like that. I'm like the crack-pusher of ice cream. I introduced them to something better than the organic brown stuff, and when they tasted real food, they only wanted to eat that.

The same thing is true with grace. Once you taste grace, rules and legalism and law will make you sick, and you will run away from it. As a college student, I remember experiencing genuine worship for the first time. Even though as a teenager I had been in a great church with a dynamic student ministry, I had never really experienced authentic worship. Then, years later, at a retreat I led as a youth pastor, we experienced a real mighty move of the Lord. I remember thinking, *I can never go back and enjoy business as usual ever again.* The same

> Once you taste grace, rules and legalism and law will make you sick.

thing is true when you see grace in action for the first time.

The Problem

As a pastor, I've heard this phrase regularly, "Pastor, I just can't live the Christian life."

To which I respond with the question, "Well, what does it mean to live the Christian life?" I mean, really? What does that mean?

How would you respond to that question?

People's answers, more often than not, include the idea that living the Christian life means making God number one in their lives.

But what does making God number one in your life really mean? Some say it means to do what Jesus would do in every situation. The problem with that answer is everyone who tries it eventually comes to the conclusion that it's impossible to know how to respond like Jesus in all situations. For example, some people encounter situations at work that are too hard to handle the way Jesus would. There's always that person in the office that makes it seem impossible to control what you say when that person is around. Or there's that woman who always dresses immodestly, so it's a daily battle to keep your eyes to the ground when she walks by.

Others may not struggle at work, but they might say, "If Jesus was married to my spouse, I'm not sure even He would know what to do."

What people don't realize is when they answer the question, "What does it mean to live the Christian life?" is that they are encapsulating their views of Christianity. Many times what people answer is what they're living out in their own lives, convinced they have accurately diagnosed their problems, and through their diagnosis, they know the correct answer.

Copycats

Here's the thing: God doesn't want to be number one in your life. He wants to *be* your life. In fact, the pursuit of trying to make Him number one in your life could be part of your problem, or it may even be the reason that you haven't broken through your problems. God doesn't want to just be in front of everything in your life. He wants to *be* everything.

I know that the guy who invented the WWJD bracelets did well, and it challenged a lot of Christians to think before acting. But ultimately, everyone who tries to live a perfect life as Jesus did will be frustrated.

Why?

We're human. We make mistakes. We don't know everything. No human is capable of being able to approach every situation and scenario in life and know exactly what Jesus would do.

But that's the thing—God never asked you to be a copycat of Jesus. God wants to be your whole life. Acts 17:28 KJV says, "In him we live, and move, and have our being." That's pretty much all of our life, right? Living, moving, and having our being. Philippians 1:21 says, "To live is Christ." Again, in Colossians 3:4, it tells us that Christ is our life.

There are different meanings to saying someone is number one in your life. For example, I could say that my wife, Meredith, is my number-one love (you can put whatever word in there depending on how strange you are—my number-one honey, my number-one sweetie, my number-one lover, etc.). Now, if I meant that she's the only one, I'm in safe territory. But if I meant she's number one, but this other girl is number two, and this one is number three, etc., I'm in big trouble, right?

The same applies to Jesus Christ. If you say that living the Christian life is making Him number one above everything else, then He is not your life. God wants to be the only one. He wants to be your life.

I realize there are those of you who will read this and think, *Sorry, but that's too tall of an order to fill. I've got too many other things in my life right now that are important. Plus, isn't it kind of selfish for God to want to be everything? Doesn't He realize I have to commit to more than just Him?*

My challenge to you: Give God a chance. I know it defies logic, but before you give up and decide this is too hard of a commitment, give God a chance to prove it's the best decision you could ever make.

After all that we've worked through together, consider that some of your ideas about the Christian life may not be grounded in the Bible at all. Consider that what you've thought living for God is about possibly isn't even true. Maybe it's time to give God a chance to prove Himself—without the influence of others' actions and words.

What if the Christian life is completely different than anything you have ever imagined or known? What if what the Bible says is really true, and what people have led you to believe is really false?

I believe the grace of God is bigger than any of us have ever given it credit. But in order to appreciate God's grace, we must be willing to admit that we don't currently have everything correctly sorted out in our belief systems.

It's like the two guys who went fishing. One guy kept throwing the big fish back in the water, so his friend asked, "Why are you throwing the big ones back?"

He responded, "They won't fit in my frying pan."

That's exactly how a lot of people determine whether or not God should be their everything. They say, "I can't understand a God like that. And since He doesn't fit in my brain, I don't want to be bothered with that big of a truth. I'm just going to stick to following things that I can sort out and that will help get me through tomorrow." But you're missing out on the big fish.

> In order to appreciate God's grace, we must be willing to admit that we don't currently have everything correctly sorted out in our belief systems.

No Fillers

My favorite meal, bar none, is beef filet. I like a rib eye, but it usually has too much fat. I think the flavor is good, but because of the fat, I end up spitting it out, which is frowned upon when you're in a fancy steakhouse.

There's one place in Tulsa that's my favorite, and it serves a filet with the bone in. This concept is straight from the hand of God—don't leave the bone in the rib eye because the rib eye already has enough flavor from the fat. But leave the bone in the filet so you get the flavor of a rib eye but the texture of a filet. Remarkable!

One of the reasons I love this steakhouse is because of the way they handle the entire dining experience. Some steakhouses have this concept of giving you a bucket of peanuts before you eat and they entertain you with the freedom of throwing the shells on the floor. I don't feel any more free throwing the shells in a bucket than I do throwing them on the floor, but some drunken guy in a creative meeting came in and said that it's a marketing tactic—just let the people throw them on the floor. Some states don't allow it anymore because of health codes, so when you end up in a state that allows it, you're like "This must be grace!"

But what happens after you've eaten a whole bucket of peanuts? When the real food, the filet, comes to the table and you're already full and you're not really as interested in the filet as you could have been—God's gift to diets, right?

Could this be the problem with our perception of God as well? We fill ourselves up on the culture we live in, then when we hear teachings about God, we're so full of those cultural peanuts that we don't really have an appetite anymore. When it comes time for the filet and for us to allow God to be our everything, we can't even grasp our need for God because of the garbage we've already consumed.

It may be time to do a cleanse—I'm not talking about lemonade or juice. Take some time to cleanse your mind, your attitude, your beliefs. Give yourself a clean slate by dismissing what you've heard before. Give Him a chance to be your everything.

New Questions

For those of you who have already surrendered to God, you may need a cleanse as well—a cleanse of your belief system. Is God number one in your life, or is He the only one? If you, also, have a hard time grasping the idea of making God everything, then I would challenge you to cleanse your thinking with these two questions:

1. What do I believe?
2. What does the Bible say?

It's important to regularly ask yourself what you believe because *all of us* have been born into a world system in which every major religion and system known to man stresses our responsibility to stay in favor with God through a specifically designated list of things that you *will* and *will not* do. But those works are not equal with God. God needs to be your everything first.

I realize it is a major paradigm shift to embrace the idea that God and good works are not on equal levels of importance. The Bible clearly outlines that your behavior has absolutely nothing to do with gaining or staying in favor with God. For many, if not all, of you, that's a big jump, and I know that it may take some time to pry your fingers off the list of good works you've come to embrace wholeheartedly.

But before you throw this book aside and strut off with your list of good works clasped tightly in your fist, take a moment and ask yourself the second question: What does the Bible say? Most people would swear the essence of biblical Christian living is finding out what the Bible says and then doing it. They strive and strive and strive to live by the Bible's

> Becoming a Christian has nothing to do with you trying.

lists of dos and don'ts. They believe that they are going to heaven because they have spent their life following those lists.

But trying to live the Christian life is the equivalent to trying to become a Christian. Becoming a Christian has nothing to do with you trying. You don't believe me? Read the Bible. When you evaluate what you believe based on what the Bible says, you will find real truth . . . and a whole lot of grace.

Study the Real Thing

When an FBI agent or a banker is trained to identify counterfeit money, he doesn't study counterfeit bills. Instead he sits in a room with white walls, a table and chair, and real monetary bills to study and examine. Why? If he knows the real thing, he'll be able to identify a counterfeit when it comes along.

It's the same with religion. Don't spend your time examining different people's lists of dos and don'ts. Study the real thing. Get to know what the Bible says. When you know the Bible, then you will be able to recognize when false teaching and false doctrines come along in your life.

Religion has painted God in a falsely mean way, which causes us to believe that we can't approach Him in a moment of need. But those are the times when God *wants* to be approached.

Look at the Scriptures. God wants us to be able to approach Him and come to Him when we have a need. He wants to give us grace. When you begin to take what you've been taught and what you've believed and see what the Word says about it, the truth will quickly prevail. In fact, usually grace is so misunderstood that if people actually studied what the Bible says about it, they'd think the Bible was wrong. Yeah, it's that different.

Welcome to a New Place

Going back to the children of Israel—later in their journey to the Promised Land, God instructs them to follow the Levites who are carrying the ark of the covenant. The ark was a guide in their journey, and Joshua explains why it was necessary in Joshua 3:4 (NIV): "Then you will know which way to go, since you have never been this way before."

"You have never been this way before" is a truth many of us have not comprehended in our walks with God. Perhaps it's one of the greatest understatements of the Bible. When we walk in true grace—grace as the Bible defines it—we find we're on a path we might never have set foot on before. It is in this new territory that our sense of dependence on God and His grace becomes so necessary. When we don't or can't rely on our experience and knowledge and must depend on Him, then He really becomes God in our lives.

When it happened to the Israelites, they were moving into Canaan; and similar to a Christian moving from the wilderness of religion into a place of grace, they found life changed completely. To live in grace is to experience the reality of who we are in Jesus Christ all the time. It's like going from a one-dimensional viewpoint to a four-dimensional viewpoint. It's not just black ink on white pages anymore. It's real and live and big. And it changes all of your life.

Study Questions

1. Give an example of a religious belief that you followed and later realized wasn't true.

2. What are five words or phrases that you would use to describe God and where they might be found in the Bible.

3. List five token worldly "fillers" that consume your thought life. What are some practical steps you can take to reduce those "fillers" so that you can know more of what the Bible has to say?

Chapter Six

The Religion of Legalism

I don't think Jesus hates religion. I think church is there for those who need it. A wise pastor once said to me that people usually show up in church because they either have something to celebrate or they are hurting and need something concrete to lean against. Sometimes they stay for a while, sometimes they get what they need and pass on by, and sometimes they go in and out like I do. In the end, isn't it what we do with our lives outside of the church that really matters?

—C. B. [Excerpted from www.jesushates religion.com message board]

The world is full of catchphrases that we treat as rules for living but are not found in the Bible. For example, where is this principle in the Bible: "God helps those who help themselves"?

Yeah, it's not anywhere in the Book. Do we really believe that God *only* helps people who can help themselves? What about the helpless? Do we think God looks at them and says, "Sorry, I can't help you; you didn't follow the rule. You didn't help yourself."

Legalism isn't the use of rules and laws. It's the misuse of rules and laws. Let's look at some other rules we play by.

Often, our culture's rules come in the form of platitudes. "Nice guys always finish last." Really? I don't believe this. I'm a nice guy. And sometimes I don't finish last. "The enemy of my enemy is my friend." I'm not so sure. Maybe the enemy of my enemy should be my enemy too!

Because the Bible is moral in nature, sometimes we are bound to inaccurate theology for the same reason we adopt the rules of our culture: we seldom examine the rules that govern our lives. Every Christian should examine the content and the source of their theology, though sadly, we rarely do. For example, somewhere the idea that a believer can lose their salvation snuck its way into the church. Actually, this one really ticks me off. Why? Well, first of all, you did nothing to earn it.

To say you can lose your salvation is like me saying to my dad, "I don't want to be your son anymore. I want my DNA and name changed." Would that really make any difference? Did I ever have a say in being a part of the family I was born into? No. I didn't earn my way into my family; therefore, I can't revoke my blood at any given moment.

Assuming you can do something to lose your saving relationship and knowledge of Jesus Christ, implies that you did something to get it. But you didn't do something to get it. He *gave* it to you as a free gift.

Here's another principle people live by that really bothers me: "What I do (i.e., my good works) helps me gain favor with God."

I'm telling you right now, we have to shake that belief off like a dog coming out of a lake. It's legalism.

Legalism is the system of living in which we try to make spiritual progress or gain God's blessing based on what we do. But you'll never find that principle as a requirement for salvation in the Bible.

I love Matthew 11:28: "Come to me, all of you who are weary and carry heavy burdens, and *I will give you rest*" (emphasis mine). God didn't call us to follow a large list of processes that will earn us greater favor in

His eyes. He says He's called us to rest—to live a life of peace.

Does This Match?

Salvation, this journey God created, is not about imitation. It's about habitation. It's about God making His habitat in you. It's about God living through you. That's it.

Do you believe you can do more to gain favor with God?

Yes? Then my next question is simply, "What does the Word say?"

As you evaluate what you believe and compare it to the Word of God, you have to figure out if your beliefs and the Word stand together.

Fact-Check Everything

I didn't just make up this concept. The Bible tells us to check everything with the Word. Even Paul and Silas from the Bible, great teachers and men of God, had their teachings carefully scrutinized against the Word of God: "They searched the Scriptures day after day to see if Paul and Silas were teaching the truth" (Acts 17:11).

I'm telling you, if they had to check up on Paul and Silas, you had better check up on me. And you should check any community group leader, Bible teacher, or pastor who teaches you. No one is exempt from this process—Billy Graham, Mother Teresa, etc. We're all human. Only God's Word is infallible. It is the only standard.

No truth is new truth. There's no such thing. But there are truths that need to be newly realized by followers of God—truths previous generations understood, but have since been forgotten. The Bible says, "You will know the truth, and the truth will set you free" (John 8:32).

Before you adjust your belief system, be absolutely sure of what the Bible says. The Bible, not religious indoctrination or a word someone prophesies over you, has to be your map. Only the Bible is completely trustworthy. Live your life where anything you've been taught is fair game to scrutiny.

> Live your life where anything you've been taught is fair game to scrutiny.

I know of a pastor who had a conversation with a guy who was considering joining his church. The man came up after the sermon and asked the pastor what he believed about such-and-such doctrine. The pastor told what he believed and then showed him where it could be found in the Bible. Then the guy argued, "Well, that's not what I believe."

"Well, what do you believe?" the pastor asked.

"I believe what my church believes," he stated and he named the church.

So the pastor said, "Okay, what does your church believe?"

And he said, "What I believe."

The pastor asked, "Well, what do both of you believe?"

Answer . . . "The same thing."

Blindness like that, caused by religion, can be a life-long disease. If you don't let the Great Physician come and cut away those things that are not a part of what He wants for you as His child, they will begin to grow and cloud your ability to see the Truth.

Credit, Please

As Christians, we all want to live a godly life. But the mistake comes when we believe our righteousness is determined by the way we live.

Our righteousness is determined by God because He gives us His righteousness. The Bible says it is "imputed" (which means it's credited) to those who find their way into the person of Jesus Christ (Rom. 4:24 KJV).

The moment you choose to take God's path and make Jesus the Lord of your life, your spirit is made new—that's what the Bible teaches. When you come to Jesus and believe on Him, you are made perfect and complete. Those aren't just catchy ideas. They are truths you will find in the Word of God.

God's grace is another principle that has been grossly misrepresented. What most people believe about God's grace and what the Bible actually says about it are usually two vastly different concepts. Just because you may have grown up going to church doesn't necessarily guarantee you know the grace the Bible teaches.

When I was growing up, I always heard *grace* defined as God's favor to undeserving sinners. As a teenager in youth group, I learned it as an acronym: GRACE = God's Riches At Christ's Expense. Those both sound great, and maybe you've heard those definitions too, but are they something that the Bible backs up?

Galatians, one of the books of the New Testament, is a great place to start when studying God's grace. In this book, the apostle Paul is writing to the Galatians, addressing issues that arose because both Jews and Gentiles (non-Jews) were converting to Christianity.

Originally, the Gentiles were not included by Jewish Christians and were considered outside the church—salvation was only for the Jews, in other words. After Jesus rose from the dead, it became clear that salvation was available to anyone (Acts 15).

Enter the Jewish religious leaders. They didn't have a problem with the Gentiles converting to their faith, but they rankled when the Gentiles didn't find it necessary to follow their religious customs and laws too. They basically argued, "It's fine you gave your life to Jesus, but now you have to follow the law. Those of you who were never Jewish to begin with must now follow the Jewish law and then you can become a Christian." In a nutshell, they were adding a bunch of rules to the message of grace. So, when Paul addressed the Galatians, he told them that they couldn't mix grace and law.

We can't either. Grace and works are exclusive of one another. They're like water and oil. One repulses the other:

> I am shocked that you are turning away so soon from God, who called you to himself through the loving mercy of Christ. You are following a different way that pretends to be the Good News but is not the Good News at all. You are being fooled by those who deliberately twist the truth concerning Christ.

> Let God's curse fall on anyone, including
> us or even an angel from heaven, who preaches
> a different kind of Good News than the one
> we preached to you. I say again what we have
> said before: If anyone preaches any other Good
> News than the one you welcomed, let that per-
> son be cursed. (Gal. 1:6–9)

Talk about extreme. Listen, Paul was not accusing
them of changing churches. He was accusing them of
abandoning the grace of God and going their own way.
Verse 7 even says they were perverting the grace of
God. To pervert something is to divert it to a wrong
end or purpose.

That's exactly what these religious leaders were
doing—taking God's grace and wrongly turning it back
to the law. Paul warned the Galatians not to allow that
happen in their own lives. These verses serve as a warning not to let the same happen to us.

Mixing grace and the law will bring trouble. In the
Bible, the word *trouble* comes from a Greek word, *thlip-
sis*, which literally means perplexity, confusion, and
unrest, so when someone goes back to the law by trying
to earn favor through good works, they're going to face
perplexity, confusion, and unrest.[5]

Two other times this same form of the word *trouble*
is used in Scripture. The first time is when the disciples

are in a boat and a huge storm comes. The Bible says they were greatly, greatly troubled—so much so that they feared for their lives (Matt. 14:26). The second time it's used is when King Herod is troubled to hear that baby Jesus has been born (Matt. 2:3). Quite honestly, at that point he became crazy. Well, maybe he already was, but he became fully crazed with hatred at that time. Neither instance offers any nice or favorable view of the trouble that following the law brings.

Cling to Grace

True grace, God's grace, leads to peace. That's why Paul puts them together in this introduction, "Grace and peace to you" (Gal. 1:3 NIV). In fact, that's the introduction to almost all of his letters in the Bible. He's emphasizing that a person is saved by grace but also has to live by grace.

> A person is saved by grace but also has to live by grace.

Look at 1 Corinthians 15:10, "But whatever I am now, it is all because God poured out his special favor on me." Paul identifies exactly where the grace came from—God alone. He goes on to say, "And not without results. For I have worked harder than any of the other apostles."

This may tempt you to argue, "Wait! That sounds like works." But watch what Paul says next,

"Yet it was not I but God who was working through me by his grace."

Listen, just because a church, religion, or ministry is popular doesn't mean that it's blessed by God. Even if that church or ministry performs unbelievable signs and wonders, it doesn't prove that it is operating under God's guidance. A church that is following God's only path is faithful to teach the Word of God.

Anything added to this is false doctrine. In Galatians 1, Paul is saying that those who bring false doctrine should be dedicated to destruction. When Paul wrote this, he was dealing with people adding the words of Moses to the gospel; but in our day, people are adding a whole list of rules to the gospel, which puts believers in confusion and unrest and perplexity. That's false doctrine.

Freedom

Read John 3 (the fourth book of the New Testament). All of it. The most famous verse in the New Testament is John 3:16, but it's the eighteen verses that surround it that you really want to focus on. When we're born again, we are children of the King. We are set free.

We've been redeemed and purchased by Christ. We're no longer in bondage to sin or human religious systems:

> For God loved the world so much that he gave his one and only Son, so that everyone who believes in him will not perish but have eternal life. God sent his Son into the world not to judge the world, but to save the world through him.
>
> There is no judgment against anyone who believes in him. But anyone who does not believe in him has already been judged for not believing in God's one and only Son. (John 3:16–18)

> So Christ has truly set us free. Now make sure that you stay free, and don't get tied up again in slavery to the law. (Gal. 5:1)

> So if the Son sets you free, you are truly free. (John 8:36)

Justified

Justification. The Bible teaches that the moment you enter God's path, you are justified. I always remember justification this way:

> Justified = Just As If I Never Sinned.

There are three truths about justification that every follower of Christ should understand:

Number one, justification is an act—not a process—once and for all, just as if I never sinned. This isn't an ongoing journey in our lives. There are other words like glorification, sanctification, etc., that happen along the way or one day when we get to heaven. God is working out those things in our lives on a constant basis, but justification can't be ongoing. It's done. Romans 5:1 says we have been once-and-for-all justified by faith, so we have peace with God.

Second, justification is of God. It's not the result of man's character or his works. Read that again—justification is not a result of man's character or works; it's of God. Romans 8:33 says that it is God who justifies. God. Period. God declared the sinner righteous. That's what leads to the changed life. Some may ask, "What about James 2 and the works he mentions?" Listen, as I told you before, the law was given to *reveal* sin, not *redeem* it. It's the changed life of the believer that comes from God that leads to that life that James mentions.

Finally, justification is an act of God for sinners. Romans 4:5 says that God justifies the ungodly. It's not *forgiveness* God gives us, because a person can be forgiven and go sin again and be guilty again. It's not pardon either. A criminal can be pardoned, but that criminal still has a record. That's not what God does. He justifies us—just as if I never sinned. Justification is a complete act of God for sinners. Take that truth and run with it.

Work It Out

After studying what the Bible has to say, it's clear what God's definition of grace is—it's His offer of salvation. Take it or leave it. Anyone who adds to it is creating false doctrine. Anyone who subtracts from it is shirking God's promise of justification. The Bible gives a place for good works, but they have nothing to do with being saved. That's all God.

Perhaps this truth is new to you. Can you wrap your mind around it? Can you leave behind what you've been taught previously and cling only to the Bible? You see, you don't need to become more righteous. All the righteousness, purity, and completion you've ever needed is already in you. God deposited it in you when you surrendered to Him. You just need to bring it into the reality of your everyday life.

You are righteous. So, now, live righteous.

Paul says it like this, "Work out your salvation with fear and trembling" (Phil. 2:12 NIV). What's already done on the inside of you—work it out through your lifestyle. Work it out in your thoughts and speech and actions. He doesn't say work *for* it. He says to work it out. What's already done in you—let that come out.

Some people I know would say, "This is a big truth and, quite honestly, it's confusing." In order to understand it, you're going to have to leave the other side of the Jordan. You need to have both feet planted in the same place. You can't be on both sides. You can either be on the side where God destined you to live in this grace place, or you can be on the side of rules and religion. But you can't mix them. And you've got to quit trying.

The Challenge

Examine your own walk with God and face the reality that legalism can creep into any Christian's life, and then ask yourself these questions:

1. Are you walking daily in the freedom of grace? In other words, are you free to enjoy God and free to become what He has determined you to be?
2. Are you trying to mix law and grace? *Law* means you believe you must do something in order to please God. *Grace* means the work is finished

for you (i.e., church membership and the disciplines of the faith have a place, but they are an expression of your faith; they are not added to your faith). So, do you love Jesus *because* He saved you, lives in you, and lives through you; or do you love Jesus *so that* He will live in and through you?

3. Have you been saved by the grace of God, or do you trust your morality/good works/religion/Bible? If you trust any of the latter, you're not saved; and you need to enter into a lifesaving relationship with Jesus Christ.

Study Questions

1. How does the truth that God lives in you change the way you live your life?

2. Name two good works you've done at some point in your life because you thought it was going to earn you favor with God.

3. What do you believe is the basis for God accepting you?

4. What is the truth that you learned about justification?

5. What are the areas in your life where you tend to live by rules or regulations rather than the grace of God?

Chapter Seven

The Religion of Inferiority

I saw the billboard (www.jesushatesreligion.com) today, and I agree—I grew up going to church; I was taught all the rules; and I followed them. It wasn't until I moved away from home that I discovered a bit of grace, but the rules were engrained. I couldn't help it. I was always working for my salvation, even after I was saved, maybe even some today even though I'm in my late thirties. I went to Bible college, became a Bible teacher, and I was a part of the problem. I would teach grace and rules, in other words, religion. I'd get caught up in being good rather than just being. Religion has screwed me up—from growing up with the rules, to listening to preachers preach the rules, to seeing them break the rules. Rarely did I see or feel the love from leaders. Can we just say, Pharisee?

It's the real people, the normal, those who don't get caught up in religion that I admire. I believe religion has messed up a lot of people. Those that keep the church at arm's length seem to be more normal. They don't take church too seriously. Their relationship with God and Jesus—yes, they take that serious.

I hope I wasn't a Pharisee when I was a Bible teacher, but I think, at times, perhaps I was. Today, my church has politics. If you're not in the "in crowd," it's not easy to be a teacher. You have to play the religion game to be involved—say the right things, be religious. I've seen this in every church I've ever been a member of. I don't play those games anymore. I don't care. I don't have time for it. I'm actually sick of it. I want to be involved, but I can't play the game of religion. Also, no preaching at me. I've forgotten more of the Bible and religion than most people know.

—Anonymous [Excerpted from www.jesus hatesreligion.com message board]

I will never forget a conversation I had years ago with a teenage girl at a youth camp. After one of the services, there were kids sitting around the stage area in groups of two or three asking the adult leaders for advice. This girl, we'll call her Savannah, came up to me and asked me to sit and talk with her.

Savannah was feeling overwhelmed and stressed and overweight. She didn't feel significant or valued. She even admitted that she had tried to commit suicide at one point. So I asked her this question, "Savannah, on a scale of 0 to 10, where do you think you are in terms of God accepting you?"

I'll never forget her response because she thought about it for two or three minutes. (In a scenario like that, two to three minutes of silence is powerful.) Finally, she admitted she felt like she was a three—she believed God accepted her only 30 percent of the time.

What's Your Rating?

What if I asked you the same question? On a scale of 0 to 10 in terms of God accepting you, where would you stand?

Take some time to really think about it.

If you find yourself answering with anything less than a ten, then, Houston, we have a problem! Anything less than a ten means it will be impossible for you to be truly intimate with God.

Human psychology teaches that we reject those who reject us. We run to those who accept us. This means if you don't see yourself as fully accepted by God, you're never going to be intimate with Him

> If you don't see yourself as fully accepted by God, you're never going to be intimate with Him because you don't trust Him.

because you don't trust Him. You will ultimately reject God because you believe He rejects you.

Not many Christian leaders will be that black and white, and most gloss over this truth with a message about God's unconditional love. But if you believe God doesn't accept you 100 percent of the time, the truth is you'll never be able to receive that unconditional love. If God's love is not returned, He will not force it on you: it has to be accepted. Until you understand that, inferiority will remain one of the Devil's most effective tools for messing up your life.

New I.D.

I once read about a hypnotist that came to an elementary school for an assembly—I am not sure what kind of assembly that was, but I know I've never been to one like that. We had assemblies at my school, but we never had a hypnotist. I think I would remember that . . . Wait! Or would I?

This hypnotist called four volunteers onto the stage, and he hypnotized them. Each volunteer was told that he or she was going to start acting like a different animal when the hypnotist snapped his fingers. One would be a dog, one a monkey, one a cow, and one a cat. Sure enough, when he snapped his fingers, those kids started acting like their respective animals—hopping all over the place imitating each animal's behavior. Later these children returned to their seats while their peers were still pointing and laughing. I don't think they ever fully understood what had happened.

How many Christians do we know (perhaps you've been victim to this as well) who behave in ways they don't understand? We're told we're supposed to be one thing—holy, a saint, a masterpiece of God—yet we run around awkwardly trying to duplicate the motions and behaviors that we perceive that thing to be. Granted, we all want to be saints, but we think it's too hard. We want to be holy, but we think far too much effort is required for that. And we never acknowledge the fact that it's not about imitation; it's about who God transformed us to be on the inside.

Most of the time I hear the excuse, "Pastor, I just can't be a perfect Christian. It's easier just to be myself." Okay, well, what does it mean to "be yourself"? You may say you're a Christian, but do you realize how much your identity changed when you became one? (More on that later.)

Most of us have accepted this false identity—a false concept of what a Christian looks and acts like—because of the power of suggestion from the world, from the Devil, or from our own logic. But who are you? Who does the Bible say you are? The truth is you can never consistently behave in a way that is different than the way you see yourself, so it's time to start seeing yourself the way God sees you.

Funhouse Mirrors

Have you ever been in a carnival or maybe a haunted house that included a hallway of distorted mirrors? Each mirror is bent so your reflection is distorted crazily. Looking in the mirror, all of a sudden you have a very large forehead and a tiny mouth. It's hilarious and a little bit disturbing at the same time. Then there are the ones we hope are in there—the ones that make your stomach disappear by stretching your body to look tall and skinny.

No matter how much time you spend in front of those mirrors and no matter how pleasing or displeasing your reflections are, they are never going to reflect the real you.

Religion acts as a distorted mirror. It exaggerates your good deeds, yet it minimizes your faith to an indistinguishable wavy line. Your focus shifts to good works.

Religion deceives us by making us believe we can only come to God when we have it all together or when our good deeds stack up enough. The Devil wants Christians to believe God will only accept people when they're faultless. And even though the Bible teaches that once people are saved, they're in Christ; the Devil tries to convince believers that being in Christ is insufficient. Satan wants everyone to buy into the lie that one must be flawless and faultless in order to make it to heaven.

> Religion deceives us by making us believe we can only come to God when we have it all together or when our good deeds stack up enough.

Do you know why Satan uses that strategy? He understands the crucial principle that if you don't see yourself fully accepted by God, you can never be intimate with Him. It is ignorance of this truth that has crippled many Christians from enjoying the blessed life God has promised to all who follow Him. Plus, if you don't see yourself the way God sees you, you will never behave consistently with the Bible. And that's just what doubters want to see—a hypocrite whose life justifies why they shouldn't follow God.

The Religion of Inferiority

Inferiority is acting or performing in a way that is comparatively poor or mediocre to who one really is. It comes about when a person doesn't see himself correctly. Most Christians I know have either knowingly or unknowingly bought into this man-made path that leads to nowhere. They act and live and perform in a way that is mediocre compared to what God has called them to.

We've already talked about asking yourself two important questions when dealing with religion: What do I believe? What does the Word say? I hope you've been asking yourself these questions as you've been reading this book, and my prayer is that throughout your life you will take any new teaching or message and compare it to what the Word says before you put your trust in it.

When we look to the Word to see what it says about inferiority, we find that who we are as children of God was *given* to us. God never intended for us to be repressed. God wants us to be released. He wants us to be liberated to discover and to live out our roles and purposes in life (Rom. 8:1–2; John 8:36).

People who are living in inferiority believe God approves of them because they are humble enough to admit (sometimes even brag) that they fall short of God's standards. They live their lives with one purpose—doing what is in their power to close the gap between God and them—convinced God is pleased based on the effort they are making.

Need-to-Know Basis

Next to having a knowledge of God, knowing who you are in Jesus may be the most important thing you come to understand as a Christian. As a believer and as a child of Christ, this is one of the biggest truths you must accept.

> Freedom comes with the truth.

Jesus said when you know the truth, it will set you free (John 8:32).

Freedom and truth work together. Freedom comes with the truth. Freedom comes in the Person who is the truth—the way, the truth, and the life—the person of Jesus Christ (John 14:6). So what is the truth?

Culture Shock

Most Christians have a spiritual inferiority complex. They see themselves as a saved sinner who's just trying their best to live for God. Sounds noble, right? But is it biblical?

Nope.

So why does it sound so right?

Because it's something culture has been ramming down our throats since we were born. Let's play a little game. Fill in the blanks:

Lebron James is a _____.

Bono is a _____.

Tom Hanks is an _____.

Do you see it? Our culture creates identity based on behavior: Lebron James is a basketball player; Bono is a singer; Tom Hanks is an actor. Our identities are determined by how we behave. We define who we are based on what we do.

> While our culture may define identity based on behavior, the truth of the matter is behavior does not determine identity.

I could meet you on the street, shake your hand, and ask, "Who are you?" You'd tell me your name first, but if I asked you to tell me about yourself, you'd immediately default to explaining what you do. That's the answer we figure people are looking for when they ask that question. That's where we believe our identities lie. While our culture may define identity based on behavior, the truth of the matter is behavior does not determine identity.

Birthmarks

What determines identity according to the Bible? Birth.

Birth determines identity. That's the reason the scriptural terms *new birth* and *born again* are such big deals in the kingdom of God. We Christians are born again when we surrender our lives to God.

Behavior doesn't determine identity. Birth does. I was born a human. My DNA says I'm a human, so I am a human. My behavior doesn't determine that.

Throughout this chapter, I'm going to give you a lot of Scripture. Circle them. Highlight them. Write them down on a separate sheet of paper—whatever it takes for you to know what the Word says. I can't do this for you.

Okay, let's start with 2 Corinthians 5:17, "If anyone is in Christ, he is a new creation; the old has gone, the new has come!" (NIV). Those who become Christians— those who are born again—become new people. They're not the same anymore. This verse tells us the old life is gone, and a new life has begun.

Think about it. What's the root word of *creation?* Create.

When you create something, you form it out of nothing. When God created you, He did not improve upon you. He made you new. You are not a better version of the one you were before. You are not even the same person you were before you came to Jesus Christ. You are a *new* creation. You're born again—new.

> When God created you, He did not improve upon you. He made you new.

When you became a Christian, quite honestly, you became a spiritual being for the first time. You had no spiritual identity before you were in Christ because your spirit was dead. It had no life. But when you came to Jesus, you became alive spiritually. God's Holy Spirit now lives inside of you.

Life I.D.

Like God, you are a triune being. You are a body, a soul, and a spirit. The body is our sense of consciousness that relates to the five senses. The soul is our mind, will, and emotions—our personality. Our spirits were dead when we were born in the world, and when we became Christians and gave our lives to Jesus, we became alive through a new birth. The essence of our true identities is found in our spirits.

To put it all together, you are a spirit that has a soul that lives in a body. So your identity can only be found at the level of the spirit. This is why non-Christians are working so hard to make a mark on this world. They don't have a spiritual identity; all they have is what they do between birth and death.

Christians are different. We will never be satisfied with our identity if we only look to our accomplishments between birth and death (i.e., body level). Our identity will never be found at the level of soul either. It has to be found at the level of spirit. In fact, that doesn't just apply to Christians—everyone's identity lies in their spirits whether they acknowledge it or not.

Ephesians 2:10 says, "For we are God's workmanship, created in Christ Jesus to do good works, which God prepared in advance for us to do" (NIV). God has brought to life those who were dead in sin. So our identity is now *in Christ*.

Acts 17:28 says, "'For in him we live and move and have our being.' As some of your own poets have said,

'We are his offspring'" (NIV). That's all of life—living, moving, having our being, right?

Colossians 3:4 continues this theme by saying, "And when Christ, who is your life, is revealed to the whole world, you will share in all his glory." Christ is everything.

Sinners Forever?

Now, this raises a great question. If the old man (our sin nature that we're born with) dies once we are saved, why do we still sin?

Great question. In order to answer that, we have to understand both who we are and where the battleground lies. Let's start with who we are.

Question: Can you, as a Christian in Christ Jesus, have the power to overcome every temptation from the time you come to Jesus and know Jesus until the day you die? Do you really have that ability?

Take a moment to think about this because your answer greatly impacts your theology.

As you think it through, it would appear that you would have to conclude yes: in Christ you have the power to overcome every temptation. That sounds great, but then you would have to admit you don't actually overcome every temptation. In fact, a closer look at your personal testimony would expose that you haven't even come close to overcoming every temptation in your life. Don't worry; you're not alone. My record's far from clean, and I'm positive we're in good company with, well, every other human on the planet.

This would lead us to conclude Christ possesses the power to overcome every temptation. That's the only reason He can be our Savior. And, yes, He is in you and in me. So, in and of myself, I don't have the ability to overcome everything, but in Jesus I do. Now that we've established that, let's move on to the battleground.

Know Your Battleground

Part of the reason Christians fall into the same sin again and again is because they don't understand the enemy's mode of operation. Unless they understand Satan's MO, they're always going to be vulnerable. Just like in times of war, when one side gets inside information about the enemy's strategy, the enemy no longer has the upper hand.

The enemy for all Christians is Satan. He and his henchmen are constantly strategizing and planning attacks against you. Satan doesn't care if you're already on God's path or if you're still searching; the Bible says he doesn't care what your position is; he's still out to destroy you (John 10:10). The good news is we already know the Devil's strategies. He doesn't have any new ideas. And when you know his moves, you can put him in checkmate every time.

When the Devil tries to attack you, he doesn't follow the rules of engagement. He doesn't come to a pre-established battlefield and wait for you to come and defend yourself. He goes for the kill every time. And he always plays by his own rules.

Thankfully, he doesn't have many strategies. There's one tactic he uses before you surrender your life to God, and there's one he relies heavily upon after you surrender your life to God.

Before you are born again, Satan knows you have a sin nature (read Romans chapter 6 and the entire book of Ephesians for more information) inside of you. That just means that no one has to teach you to do wrong; it's your nature. This is glaringly evident when you watch toddlers interacting with one another. Rarely does a parent have to teach their child the word *mine*—that word and all its ramifications are part of that child's nature. It's when the child is expected to *share* that parents have to actively engage in teaching a new behavior to their children.

But we aren't stuck with that sin nature forever. When we're saved, Ephesians 2:1–6 says our sin nature is put to death by God. In Romans 6:1–3, it says:

Well then, should we keep on sinning so that God can show us more and more of his wonderful grace? Of course not! Since we have died to sin, how can we continue to live in it? Or have you forgotten that when we were joined with Christ Jesus in baptism, we joined him in his death?

Then look at verse 6, "We know that our old sinful selves were crucified with Christ *so that sin might lose its power in our lives.* We are no longer slaves to sin" (emphasis mine).

Now, let me clear up a potentially confusing term you may encounter while studying this. The Greek word *sarx* in the New Testament is often translated incorrectly. *Sarx*, in the Greek, means flesh, but many modern-day translations sometimes use *sin nature* for *sarx*. *Flesh* and *sin nature* are two completely different elements in our lives. So sometimes when you read about the sin nature in the New Testament, it really is talking about your flesh. I'll explain more later. Stick with me.

God gives us a new nature when we're born again. That sin nature is not just gone, the New Testament says God circumcised it from us (Rom. 2:29). He cut it away. The sin nature is dead and gone and is no longer a part of our lives.

Human Default

Once we're saved and Satan can no longer rely on our sin nature to draw us toward doing wrong, then the Devil looks to his other main weapon—the flesh.

Again, Bible translations sometimes make this hard to understand—especially considering we're translating the Bible to English, one of the most difficult languages to learn because of all the inconsistencies. So keep in mind while you're reading that sometimes when the Bible uses the word *flesh*, it means skin—like the skin on a human or an animal. But most of the time, the word *flesh* is referring to the manner in which we try to do life on our own. Basically, when we allow the flesh to control us, it means we've taken the steering wheel from God and put ourselves back in the captain's chair. Our reliance has shifted from God's way to our way.

Okay, let's review.

Sin nature = what every human is born with, but it is cut away from us when we are saved.

Flesh = making decisions based on your own knowledge, not God's.

Got it?

Let's continue. Galatians 5:17 says that what the flesh wants is opposed to the spirit. (If your Bible says *sin nature* instead of *flesh*, it's an incorrect translation—see,

I told you that Greek information would come in handy.) So if what the flesh wants is opposed to the spirit—our new nature—then what the spirit wants is opposed to the flesh. Still with me?

How does this apply to your everyday life? Basically, your flesh is the reason you end up doing what you don't want to do.

Paul addressed this issue in Romans 7:15, "I don't really understand myself, for I want to do what is right, but I don't do it. Instead, I do what I hate." Paul, a great minister and man of God, known the world over for his contribution in spreading the gospel, struggled with his flesh. But does that mean he just gave into it, and let his flesh control his life? No. He used his knowledge of the flesh to strategize how he could defeat the Devil on his own turf.

When you came to Jesus, the flesh did not die. You were trying to do things your way from the time you were born and that behavior didn't just go away when you were saved. This means you must take initiative and relearn, remove, and replace those desires with truth. If you want to win, you need to retrain your brain. It won't happen automatically.

Did you catch that? It doesn't happen automatically. Paul acknowledged that his flesh was still alive and active after he got saved. And you, too, must acknowledge that your flesh is constantly trying to work against you to do the things you know you shouldn't do.

Our brains will always default to following the flesh any moment we aren't actively depending on God. If you're going to defeat the Devil, you must consciously and consistently throw aside your self-reliance and put all your trust and hope in God.

> Our brains will always default to following the flesh any moment we aren't actively depending on God.

When we're in the flesh, we depend on our own abilities to change and to be accepted by God. In our world, we tend to believe that the way to become righteous is to do righteous things. So, we try to be righteous by our own efforts. But listen; when you try to be righteous by your own effort, you are gratifying the flesh. It's sin.

There Is Hope

I know I've painted a pretty dark picture of what's warring inside of us before and after we're saved. But let me ease your mind with another truth. When a person is saved, not only is the sin nature cut away, but that person receives a new nature—one that stirs up a desire to behave in a way that brings honor to Jesus. Read that again because it's very significant—all Christians have a new nature that stirs within them a desire to behave in a way that brings honor to Jesus.

It's not just dark forces at war within you. God has equipped you with a new nature—one that longs for and desires to please Him. A nature

> All Christians have a new nature that stirs within them a desire to behave in a way that brings honor to Jesus.

that sees the emptiness that our culture has to offer, and quite frankly, is disgusted with society's measly offerings. This nature delights in doing good and following God's Word. It's a nature that smiles when someone asks, "But if I have to stop doing everything that I'm doing now, what will I have left to do?" because it knows the absolute joy and freedom that comes with salvation.

Wait, Do I Have One of Those?

I'm going to say something that is probably going to shock you. In fact, it's not something that you will hear many other religious leaders say. Brace yourself. Are you ready?

If you don't have a new nature, you are not a Christian.

I know that sounds harsh, but let me tell you about Leslie. Leslie, a young woman from the church I pastor, was recently baptized. Before she was baptized, she e-mailed me and shared some of her testimony. It began, "I was saved today" (which would have been about a week before she was baptized). She went on to explain that she grew up going to church, Christian kids' camps, youth camps, and basically any other religious function you can name. Add to this equation that she had been in my church for three years. It wasn't until she heard me teach about the religion of good works that she realized she'd had rules and religion, but she had never had a new nature.

So at the end of my message, she sat in her chair and prayed to give her life to Christ. For a grown woman who had been raised in a heavily religious setting to admit that until that point she had not been saved was a big deal. She figured telling all of her friends, who already thought she was saved, what she had done would be embarrassing, but, to her surprise, she found it was exactly the opposite.

The next day she told every single person she knew that Jesus had come in her life and her life was forever different. Why wasn't she embarrassed?

Her new nature was alive and kicking; and it was generating an eagerness to honor God with her life. Jesus set her free.

Leslie isn't the only person who has experienced this. Ask some Christians you know. Have they had similar experiences? I can guarantee they have. Now, granted, if they were saved as a young child, they may not remember what life was like before salvation; but if you ask someone who was saved when he/she was a little older, I promise their testimony will line up with Leslie's.

This means that anyone who belongs to Christ has become a new person. The old life is gone; a new life has begun! (2 Cor. 5:17).

I Feel Good

Go back to the story of the prodigal son (Luke 15:11–32). As I read that story, I can't help noticing the older brother's reaction when the younger brother comes home. Here is the older brother out in the field working and when he gets home, he hears the music and dancing. Naturally, he asks what's going on, and he's told that his brother who was gone has come home.

Plus, his dad has killed the fattened calf and put a ring on the brother's finger and a robe on his back. When the older brother hears this, the Bible tells us he is angry and refuses to go in.

It reminds me of when I was in college. While I was in school, I went to three or four Bible studies a week. The reason I did so was the very same reason my other friends went out and got drunk. We were doing what made us feel good. We were going to the places where we were affirmed and accepted. Basically, we were living by our flesh and letting what feels good dictate our life choices.

To be honest, I think going to Bible studies made me feel better than my friends who got drunk, but either way, I was doing it because it gratified my flesh. Understand, at a Christian college, the peer pressure is either in one ditch or the other. There are the rebellious flaunt-their-lack-of-new-nature-lifestyle students on one extreme, and there are the top-of-the-spiritual-food-chain-almost-holier-than-thou-but-wouldn't-ever-say-that students on the other extreme. I wanted to be part of the latter. Going to as many Bible studies as possible made me feel like I had a leg up on the other students, and I allowed that to be my reason for going to the Bible studies.

But doesn't God tell us to study the Bible?

Absolutely. And when we have that new nature, our desire to study the Bible is stirred up within. But if I were completely honest with myself at the time, I would have realized I wasn't making choices based on that new nature—I was making my decisions based on what made me feel good.

So can I change my flesh?

Let me start by saying God won't alter your flesh for you. When you were saved, God changed your spirit, but changing the flesh is up to you. The only way to alter the flesh is to change your thinking. If you fill your mind with your friends' opinions, temptations, and bitterness from hurtful past experiences, they will feed your flesh and make you more susceptible to lies. If your thinking is always negative, then that will alter your perception of reality.

Remember, you've got to understand the Devil's MO. He's banking on you feeding your flesh. He wants your perception of reality to be skewed because he knows that believing the truth makes you righteous, not your actions. But if you are always dwelling on falsehoods, you will never know the

> If you don't know the truth, you will always believe that your actions can earn your righteousness.

truth. And if you don't know the truth, you will always believe that your actions can earn your righteousness. It's a vicious circle. You've got to cling to truth like an anchor, or you'll get sucked into the centrifuge of Satan's deceptions.

Danger Ahead

Recently, I had lunch with a friend of mine, a Presbyterian pastor from my area. Originally we met because our kids were on the same athletic teams, but over time we found excuses to hang out at places that didn't involve metal bleachers. The first time just the two of us hung out, he suggested that we meet at Shiloh's, a local diner at 1:30 p.m. Now, if you know anything about my personality, you know that punctuality is good. So, I arrived early at Shiloh's, got a table, and waited for him to come.

It wasn't long before I had already had a cup of coffee, ordered my meal, and built a relationship with the waitress; but he still hadn't shown up. Finally, I texted him and asked, "Hey, are we meeting today?"

He texted back, "Yes. 1:30," which irritated me. So I texted back,

"What time do you have?"

"1:42."

"Are you here?"

"Yes."

So we both started walking around different corners of the restaurant trying to find each other. Finally, he texted me, "Go to the cash register."

I headed straight for the cash register, and he headed to the cash register; but we still couldn't find each other. Little did I know, Shiloh's has a second location about a mile down the road. So here are two pastors walking around two different Shiloh's looking for each other. I finally got in my car and drove to his Shiloh's.

At one point, we started discussing the parable of the prodigal son, and I said, "Think about your children." (He's got four boys.) "Which way would you want them to err? Younger-brother err and run off into the world of sin and unrighteousness? Or would you want them to err in self-righteousness, like the older brother?" I continued, "I'm not sure which way I'd go because there's still this legalist in me that I have to work out. The legalist in me says, if you're going to err, err in righteousness (even if it is self-righteousness) because there are scars and wounds that I was prevented from as a college kid who acted in self-righteousness."

He admitted up front he didn't know which way he'd want his kids to go, which blew me away. He went on to explain that while he doesn't want his kids dealing with unrighteous stuff like pornography or alcoholism, people who are involved in that stuff know exactly where their lives are headed. The problem with erring in self-righteousness is there's no guarantee the person sees the obstacles in their path.

When you think about the story of the prodigal son, Jesus left that story with the self-righteous one not coming to the party, but the unrighteous one being the guest of honor. The unrighteous son saw where his life was headed, very quickly, and he came to a place where he admitted he needed a savior. Whereas the self-righteousness brother was kept from having a relationship with his father, yet he was convinced he was in the right.

Whether you're caught up in self-righteousness or unrighteousness, know that the Devil's got your number. He knows that whether or not you see where your life is headed, if he can get you to live in the flesh and make decisions to take control of your life away from God, then he can keep you in a spiral of misconceptions that will destroy your quality of life. As I said before, know who you are in Christ. The Truth will set you free.

Study Questions

1. Before reading this book, what were some ways you thought a Christian should act?

2. What are some attributes of a person who is following the religion of inferiority?

3. What are some attributes of a person who knows who they are in Christ?

4. What tactics does the Devil use against you or against people you love? What are some ways that you can counter his attacks?

Chapter Eight

Please Keep Identification on You at All Times

I must admit that before this sermon series, I never made the connection (in my mind) that my spirit has been saved for eternity the moment that I accepted the Lord Jesus Christ as my Savior. I was told that but could not wrap my head around it. I'm struggling and will continue to struggle to "shake" these notions of my sin damning me forever. I'd like to thank my church (TCABC) and my pastor (Alex) for awakening me and relieving my enormous guilt and burden that religion has placed upon my shoulders since I was a little boy taking my first steps into the church that I was raised in. (It probably

should've been named Church of the Elders with raised eyebrows, guilty stares, and condemnation).
—S. [Excerpted from www.jesushates religion.com message board]

L et's backtrack a little and remember how we've gotten this far in our discussion. We started with setting the context of religion by defining it as man-made paths to God. Any man-made path to God in its simplest form is arrogance. Why? Because anytime a human being looks at the gap between God and himself and thinks, *I can fix that,* it's arrogance. The truth of the matter is that God hates it because it actually separates us from Him.

In order to get on the right path to God, the one that He made for us through the person of Jesus Christ, we have to hit some dead ends that redirect us back to God. The first dead end, one that every person must hit before believing in the salvation that God has provided, is the dead end of self. We've got to come to a place where it's all about God, where we realize there is nothing we can do that will save or redeem us. It has to be a gift from Him.

The second dead end is that of religion. When we begin to believe that from salvation to heaven it all depends on what we do to earn our way, then we have forged our own path to God and strayed from the path He created for us.

One of the religious paths people stray on is the path of legalism. Legalism is a system of living where we try to make spiritual progress or gain favor from God based on what we do. People who get caught up in legalism allow themselves to believe that their effort has a part to play in their salvation. But as we've talked about in great detail, it's only God who can save you. Only God.

Another path many stray on is that of inferiority. It's a tricky path to recognize in today's society because many times inferiority is masked in a false perception of what humility is. Many believers buy into the notion that if they think they aren't worthy, then God will accept them more. But that's so far away from the truth.

Remember, anything we believe needs to be held against the Word. If it doesn't agree with the Word, it's religion. It's not right.

Religion looks at our deeds and distorts our view of God because it focuses on our works, but that's not the life that Jesus offers us. Jesus stood against the burden of religion. His purpose was never about conforming to anything. His purpose was about transforming. Jesus never focused on the forbidden. He always focused on freedom.

May I See Your I.D., Please?

As we study Jesus' ministry on earth, we begin to see the truth about our identity in Christ. Remember, inferiority is a man-made path to God, so it's important that we know our true identity so we don't get caught up in living below our value. The religion of inferiority will rail against and pound on your true identity (as detailed in the Bible).

How will you know you've bought into the religion of inferiority? Because you will feel your identity pushing you down, keeping you from making any real progress in your journey. The religion of inferiority will blind you from who you are in Jesus. It will try to hide what you've been given and make you feel inferior to everything the Bible promises.

So, who are you?

Look to the Bible. It answers this question with three simple statements:

1. You are a saint.[7]

> To the church of God which is at Corinth, to those who are sanctified in Christ Jesus, called to be saints, with all who in every place call on the name of Jesus Christ our Lord, both theirs and ours. (1 Cor. 1:2 NKJV)

Say it to yourself, "I am a saint." Some of you may be uncomfortable saying that aloud, but the truth of the matter is you don't need to be recommended by a body of cardinals to prove that you are capable of miracles. You *are* a miracle. The dead is now alive. You have been made holy, righteous, sanctified. That's a miracle.

God *made* you holy by means of Christ Jesus just as He did all Christians everywhere. Whoever calls upon the name of the Lord Jesus Christ is a saint. Remember, you're born again. You've got a new I.D., and on that I.D. is the title "saint."

Rewind for a second. This verse was originally written to the people of Corinth. Do you know anything about the Corinthians? If you have studied them at all, you would know they certainly were not model Christians. The slogan, "What happens in Vegas stays in Vegas" started in Corinth—what happened in Corinth stayed in Corinth. Las Vegas stole that phrase.

If the Holy Spirit led Paul to write those words to the Corinthians, how much more does "called to be saints" apply to you? It's your identity. It's not based on how well you act; it's based on who you are in Jesus. And even though it may be uncomfortable to admit, it's what the Bible says.

So say it again, this time with confidence, "I am a saint." Now, if someone just heard you say that aloud, he/she may be snickering; but believe it. It's the actual truth.

2. You are God's work of art.

> For we are God's masterpiece. He has created us anew in Christ Jesus, so we can do the good things he planned for us long ago. (Eph. 2:10)

You are God's masterpiece. Another version calls you His "workmanship." In the Greek, that word is *poema*. It's where we get our word *poem* in the English language. A poem is something that a writer carefully crafts and shapes. It's something that takes time, thought, and great dedication to finish. Poets will tell you they don't just throw words down on paper and *voilà!* it's a masterpiece. They spend many hours carefully constructing and choosing each word that will bring to life their ideas and images.

God calls you His poem. You are a beautiful piece of God's poetry, His workmanship, His masterpiece. He's proud to show you off to the world. He wants others to see you and recognize His workmanship within. There's no room for inferiority when you recognize the masterpiece God has created you to be.

3. You are righteous and holy.

For the sin of this one man, Adam, caused death to rule over many. But even greater is God's wonderful grace and his gift of righteousness, for all who receive it will live in triumph over sin and death through this one man, Jesus Christ. (Rom. 5:17)

Your spirit was made righteous at salvation. (Remember, who you are on the spirit level determines your identity.) If you don't behave righteously, that doesn't change who you are. Take any one of your ordinary prince or princess movies—the boy or girl in the movie wants to act like everyone else. He/She wants to go to school, eat pizza, attend a party without a bodyguard, etc. And while they may be successful for a time, it doesn't mean they are no longer royalty. Sooner or later they are called back to their kingdom to fulfill their duties, and they must accept (and start acting like) who they really are. Their behavior never changed their identities.

> You don't have to change a thing in order to be fully accepted by God.

You're fully accepted by God whether you act like it or not: "So we praise God for the glorious grace he has poured out on us who belong to his dear Son" (Eph. 1:6). Do you understand what this means?

You don't have to change a thing in order to be fully accepted by God. It's never been based on what you do; it's based on who you are in Jesus.

No Ifs, Ands, or Especially Buts

Don't say, "But I don't feel like a saint. But I don't feel righteous or holy. But I don't feel like a work of art. I don't even feel accepted."

Let the little boy sit down, and let the man stand up. Let the little girl sit down, and let the woman stand up. You have to make a decision—are you going to live your life based on what you *feel*? Or are you going to live your life based on what the Word of God says about you? It's your choice.

Is your life going to be about faith or feelings? Faith is the only thing that pleases God (Heb. 11:6). Not your works, your faith. Satan may try to tell you that you have to *act* like a new creation, but God says you *are* a new creation.

Relax. Be yourself. It's taken care of. Now, go live life to the fullest.

Converted Worms

The person who considers himself a "sinner saved by grace" is following the religion of inferiority. He is spending his time on the defense against Satan, whereas the saint is on the offense. Those are two totally different motivations.

Don't get me wrong. I know it's common for Christians to lapse back into wrong patterns of thinking, but it's time to wake up to our true identities. Stop acting, and start living. Stop listening to the Devil's lies that you need to act better to be accepted by God. Instead, start flashing your I.D. that already proves you are a saint, masterpiece, righteous, and holy.

When we're saved, the word the Bible uses to describe what happens to us is the same word used to describe a metamorphosis. That means we are transformed—created new. None of us have ever looked at a butterfly and thought, *That's a beautiful converted worm.*[8]

Sure, that's what it is, but we don't look to the old; we look to the new. The butterfly is a new creature. You, saint, are a new creature.

> When you understand your identity, your sins will appear foolish and inconsistent with what God called you to be.

I'm not saying that by understanding your identity, it's going to cause you to live the rest of your life without sin. What I am saying is when you understand your identity, your sins will appear foolish and inconsistent with what God called you to be. This is in direct contrast with the law and religion. When you sin under the law, you feel condemned, but don't you see? That's religion. Look at what the Bible says: there is no condemnation for those who are in Jesus (Rom. 8:1).

Imputed versus Imparted

We live in a world where there are real consequences to our sins. So when those consequences take effect in our minds, it affects our identities. It's natural for that to happen, but that's why it's so important to retrain your mind. According to God, the consequence has nothing to do with your identity.

Remember Lot from the Bible? Lot ripped off his relative, Abraham, and when the choice was given to him to choose his land, he chose Sodom and Gomorrah—places God thought were so sinful He eventually burned them to the ground. Everything we read about Lot indicates Lot was sucked into the lifestyle of Sodom and Gomorrah as well, yet God still used the word *righteous* to describe Lot.

But God also rescued Lot out of Sodom because he was a righteous man who was sick of the shameful immorality of the wicked people around him. Yes, Lot was a righteous man who was tormented in his soul by the wickedness he saw and heard day after day. (2 Pet. 2:7–8)

Here's the key: in the Old Testament, God imputed righteousness to the believer. For example, He imputed it to Abraham: Abraham believed God, and righteousness was credited to him. Neither Lot nor Abraham had Jesus living inside of them like we do today, so their righteousness had to be imputed.

On the other hand, in the New Testament, not only is righteousness imputed to us, but it is also imparted. What's the difference? *Imputed* deals with legal standing; the people of the Old Testament had a righteous legal standing. *Imparted* deals with a literal event. We live in the days of grace where we are literally given the righteousness of Jesus Christ. Lot had it credited to him, Abraham had it credited to him, but you have the righteousness of Jesus *created* in you.[9] You

> We live in the days of grace where we are literally given the righteousness of Jesus Christ.

are not a converted worm. You're a butterfly—a new creation.

You're free. Not just free to live and thrive but free to make lousy choices as well. Why would anyone who has been made righteous and set free still choose to make lousy choices? It's simple. They don't know who they are. In order to do right, we have to begin to think right.

Prostitutes or Queens

Religion will never ever lead to spiritual fruit. Never. But religion will always lead to frustration. Every time.

For example, say you're a prostitute living in old English days where all of the law is decided by the king. If the king comes out with the declaration, "I forgive all prostitutes and murderers," that would be good news to you, right? Your sins are no longer credited against you. Your criminal record is torn up and thrown away. And even though that's a good thing, it's not necessarily the motivation that would cause you to change your life.

But if the king came out and said, "I want you to be my wife," now there's some motivation! Who wouldn't exchange the life of a prostitute for the life of a queen? That would be the motivation you would need to change your life.

See, most of you understand when you came to Jesus, your sins were forgiven, but that's not necessarily the motivation you need to change your behavior. It's when you realize you also became the bride of Jesus that you have the motivation to change.[10]

Hypnotic Identities

Remember when I talked about the hypnotist who performed for the fourth-graders? When those four people came out of their trances from acting like animals, they were embarrassed.

So why did they do it?

They did it because they temporarily believed a lie about their identities. Similarly, many Christians believe the lie that they must act like a holy Christian in order to please God. And, quite honestly, that's why they struggle over and over with the same sins. The deceiver has convinced them they're nothing more than sinners.

It's time to wake up, just like those hypnotized kids woke up. Wake up to who you are in Christ and what God has done in you. You're not just a sinner saved by grace. You are a saint who has the life of Jesus at the core of your being. Stop buying into the lies that cause you to act inferior to what God has created you to be. It's religion, and it does not please God.

Study Questions

1. What are some beliefs you have about yourself that are not true? What are some truths from God's Word that you might claim to overcome each of those lies?

2. What are some truths from God's Word you have a hard time accepting? Why?

3. With regard to the religion of legalism and inferiority, what are some other "religions" you see people following in an attempt to earn favor with God?

Chapter Nine

The Religion of Guilt

I was at the service Sunday, and I agree—again.

Let's say you grew up in church and were taught Quiet Time/Read Bible/Do Missions/Pray Always/ etc. and you did them out of following the "rules" because that's what Christians are supposed to do.

Much later, you want to break that—you want to stop doing the religious things for God's favor and do them because of the relationship—but following the rules are SO ingrained when I try to read Scripture. It goes back to I'm doing this to be good or maybe God will bless me for reading. I've been fighting this battle for years.

How do you change the motivation? Do you just stop doing until you want to? (BTW—if your ONLY response to this is to "pray and trust Jesus"—keep that thought to yourself.)

A consideration: Maybe legalistic types (Pharisees) should become heathens (prodigal sons) for a time so that they may truly experience grace?
—Anonymous [After listening to one of my messages about Jesus Hates Religion, this post is from the same person quoted in chapter 7.]

How many times have you been in a difficult situation where you thought, *Dear Lord! How many bad things can happen in one season of my life? I mean, when it rains, it pours.* For those of you who have dedicated your life to following God, how many times has that exasperation turned into a trip down accusation road?

Well, I have neglected my quiet time lately.

My Bible reading today wasn't that long, and it certainly wasn't that heartfelt.

I haven't prayed a whole lot recently. In fact, my prayer time has been small and miniscule.

It sounds righteous, doesn't it? Just take the blame for your sins, and then God will be impressed with your actions. But did you catch it? You've shifted the focus from God back to you again. In fact, this whole scenario is rooted in thinking that God is irritated with you because you did not do what you should've done. But you're back in religion.

The Religion of Guilt

The Devil, who loves religion, tries relentlessly to convince us we are unacceptable to God unless we are faultless. But if we are in Christ, we are faultless—that's the way Jesus sees us. In fact, that's the way God created us. But the Devil never gives up trying to convince us that if our lifestyle is not faultless, we're not acceptable to God. He tries to persuade us that being in Christ is not enough, and if you buy into that, you are giving entrance to the religion of guilt.

Think about it. Do you envision God as being tense with you most of the time? Have you reasoned God loves you only because God is love—He has to, right? No, that's guilt talking.

When you envision God Almighty as exasperated with you, you have closed the door to intimacy with Him. In essence, you are saying, "God loves me because He's bound to love. He has to love me, but He doesn't really like me."

Most believers feel that God's mood toward them at any given moment is determined by what they've done, what they do, and what they will or, quite honestly, will not do. But that's guilt. That's religion. That's not right.

Back to the Word

In the next couple of chapters, I'm going to give you a number of Scriptures to study. As I mentioned before, it would be great to go back and study those verses on your own. So as you're reading, highlight, circle, or write down the references on a separate sheet of paper so you can easily go back, study, and let them cleanse you. Ephesians 5:26 says, "That he might sanctify and cleanse it with the washing of water by the word" (KJV). It's time to clean the guilt barnacles off the ship of your soul, and the only way to do so is to know the Bible and the truth of what God says about you.

God's Children

When we look at the story of the children of Israel in the Bible, there's one point we can clearly see—they were anything but consistent. If anyone had a reason to feel guilty, it was the children of Israel.

Look at Joshua 7:1, "But the children of Israel committed a trespass in the accursed thing" (KJV). A "trespass" is a big deal. Next look at Joshua 9:14, it says, "So the Israelites examined their food, but they did not consult the Lord" (KJV). The list of inconsistencies goes on and on, yet when you read Joshua 11:23, it says God gave them the land. They were far from perfect, yet God fulfilled His promise to them anyway. They had every reason in the world to feel guilty about what they had done wrong, yet God still blessed them.

> Victory was not complete for the children of Israel because they were faultless. It was complete for them because of God and *His* faultlessness.

Victory was not complete for the children of Israel because they were faultless. It was complete for them because of God and *His* faultlessness.

Lightning-Bolt Holster

So let me just ask you this question, and I really want you to take some time to ponder it: What makes God angry?

Some people envision God up in heaven with this holster full of lightning bolts ready to be thrown when we do or do not do certain things. And even though the Bible tells us over and over and over God's *slow* to become angry (Exod. 34:6; Num. 14:18; Neh. 9:17; Pss. 86:15; 103:8; 145:8; Joel 2:13), they still believe the moment they screw up, God's ready to punish them.

In the Bible, God gets angry 153 times. And in all 153 of them, the cause of God's anger is the same—sin. God hates sin. It's the only thing that makes God angry.

Wait, you're saying God's not angry with me; but you're also saying God hates sin, and it makes him angry. So what about when I sin after my salvation? Wouldn't that make God angry with me?

Yes, if He were human. But there's a big difference between humans and God: God is not bound by time.

A Glance at Eternity

It's true that believers continue to sin. But our sins have already been dealt with in totality at the cross.

Humans are time-bound creatures. We experience reality in time parameters. In other words, reality for us is linear. There's a starting point and an ending point, and we drag time from one point to the other as we live through it. That's our reality. We live our lives and watch them play out as if they were on a time line. We look down the paths of our time lines, but we can't go back. And if you think you can, you need to lay off the drugs.

There are junctures in our lives, places where we as children were wounded by a teacher or a coach or maybe even a parent. And once we have that wound, we carry that wound through our lives. We graduate from high school, we go to college, and everywhere we are, that wound is bleeding and throbbing between our tightly gripped fingers.

Some believe marriage will make everything right, but, if you're married, you already know, marriage just magnifies the issues caused by the wound. (If you're single and think marriage will remove the issues, you're crazy. Spend a decent amount of time talking to just one married couple, and you'll quickly realize that's not true.)

Some believe all their problems will be solved when they have children. That's an even crazier thought. Like author, Kevin Lehmen, says, "I have seen the enemy, and they are small."

So people continue to move through life with their spouses and children, and they keep looking to different markers in their lives that they falsely believe will fix their problems. Life continues on a linear track; they look behind them to see the past and they look ahead to imagine the future.

But that's not the way that God sees reality. God created time. He stands above it, so He can look at it all at once. To Him there is no past, and there is no future. For God, all of it is present. He can see eternity past,

He can see eternity future, and He can see it all as one. That's the advantage of being the Creator.

So God can't be put in the same time-constraint box where you and I exist. Ecclesiastes 3:11 puts it this way, "Yet God has made everything beautiful for its own time. He has planted eternity in the human heart, but even so, people cannot see the whole scope of God's work from beginning to end." In Isaiah 46:9 it says,

> "Remember the things I have done in the past. For I alone am God! I am God, and there is none like me."

Back to the Future

Remember Enoch? God allowed Enoch to see the second coming of Christ—even though Enoch was only seven generations removed from Adam. How was this possible? God enabled Enoch to see a reality beyond time that existed already in God's eyes.

Romans 8:29–30 says,

> For God knew his people in advance, and he chose them to become like his Son, so that his Son would be the firstborn among many brothers and sisters. And having chosen them, he called them to come to him. And having called

them, he gave them right standing with himself. And having given them right standing, he gave them his glory.

These verses couldn't be true if God saw time on a linear plane like we do. He sees it all at once, and that is the reason He can give us right standing—even after we are saved and commit a sin.

Notice verse 30 says, "And having *chosen* them, he *called* them to come to him. . . . And he *gave* them right standing with himself. . . . he *gave* them his glory" (emphasis mine). This passage can be used to dissect the concept of predestination.

Does God predestine us? Of course He does. He's over all things. He sees all of it at once. But you've got to understand, it's based on the foreknowledge God has. Since He's not in the time box you and I are in, He knows there's still "whoever" in Scripture—"whoever believes in Him" (John 3:16 NKJV).

God already knows who is going to believe in Him. Of course, we make the choice to follow Him, but since He sees past and future, He already knows the choice we will make. He's not a great puppeteer pulling the strings and deciding who will be saved. He is able to view all of time as a continuum and see everything that has happened and that will happen.

Already Finished

> For God knew his people in advance, and he chose them to become like his Son, so that his Son would be the firstborn among many brothers and sisters. And having chosen them, he called them to come to him. And having called them, he gave them right standing with himself. And having given them right standing, he gave them his glory. (Rom. 8:29–30)

Let me show you five things just from the verses above that God already did for us.

1. He foreknew us. Before we were ever born, before time existed, He knew us.
2. He predestined us. He predestined us to be conformed to the image of His Son. That's what the Bible says—He chose us, all of us, ahead of time.
3. He called us. You. Me. We are all called.
4. He justified us. When the Scripture says He gave us right standing with God, that's justification. Remember, justification = just as if I never sinned.
5. He glorified us. He promised His glorification with the glorified bodies that we will get in heaven. Some people may look like they got

early dibs on their glorified bodies, but they didn't. He promised they're coming in the future.

Done, Finished, Finito

If I were to talk to my youngest son and ask him how to make a word past tense, he'd say, "Put an -ed on the end." Look back at that list of five things God's done for us—foreknew, predestined, called, justified, glorified. Paul wrote all of these things a long time ago as if they were already done. If they were past tense in Paul's time, how much more so now?

If God isn't limited by time, He can look down on our lifetime and see every sin you or I would ever commit. Then He can also take those sins and place them on Jesus who Himself bore our sin. That's the Bible, folks. He bore our sins—it's done and in the past. Look at 1 Peter 2:24,

> He personally carried our sins in his body on the cross so that we can be dead to sin and live for what is right. By his wounds you are healed.

Jesus took care of things a long time ago. It's already done.

Certificate of Debt

Not too long ago, I took my family through the Starbucks drive-thru. Usually we just order drinks, but this time everyone was really hungry and we hadn't had time to get any food from home. I let all of my kids order a drink and food knowing it would be one of the biggest bills we'd ever racked up there. When we finally pulled up to the window to pay, the barista told us that someone a couple of cars in front of us had already paid for our entire bill. Any other day that would've been a pleasant surprise, but considering this was one of the most expensive bills, we were really blessed. It felt so great to find out our bill had already been paid.

Do you know the feeling? Grab a sheet of paper and a writing utensil. Okay, now use this paper to write out your own certificate of debt. Put your name at the top and continue with this: "has committed _____ (number of) sins, and is hereby punished under the penalty of death." (The total number of sins must cover your entire life—not just the ones you've committed so far.) Okay, now sign and date the bottom.

For those of you trying to figure out how many sins to write down, it might be easier to figure an average per decade and multiply by the number of decades you plan to live. Let's say you commit an average of 500 sins per decade. Multiply that by 9 for about 4,500 sins. Next, just for the sake of making sure everything's covered, let's multiply that by 1,000. Okay, now all of the sins you could possibly commit are covered.

Now, look at Colossians 2:13–14,

> You were dead because of your sins and because your sinful nature was not yet cut away. Then God made you alive with Christ, for he forgave all our sins. He canceled the record of the charges against us and took it away by nailing it to the cross.

Did you catch it? It says God *cancelled* the record that contained all of the charges against us. He took it and destroyed it by nailing it to Christ's cross. The Greek word for cancelled is *tetelestai*. It means, "it is finished" or "paid in full." That's what Jesus said on the cross as He was dying. "Tetelestai!" He paid our debt in full.[11]

So, take a big red marker and write *tetelestai* over the front of your certificate and sign Jesus' name at the bottom. It's been paid in full. Every sin you've ever committed and all you will commit. Done. Taken care of. Keep it handy for any time someone tries to guilt you into believing all of your sins are not forgiven.

No Leftovers

Do me a favor and answer a few questions:

1. How many of your sins did God know about before you were born?
2. How many of your sins did He record on your certificate of debt?
3. How many of your sins did Jesus pay for on the cross?
4. How many of your sins was Jesus referring to when He said, "It is finished" on the cross?

Answer Key: Questions 1–4: *All of your sins.*

If that's the truth, then at the time you were saved, how many of your sins did God forgive? All. Even the ones you commit in the future.

Let's be intellectually honest, folks; would it make any sense whatsoever for God to see all of your sins, but at the moment you come to Jesus, only forgive part of them? Does that make any sense to anybody?

I grew up religious. I believed that in order to stay right with God, I had to ask for forgiveness for every single sin I committed, which scared me. I was worried and, still to this day don't understand, what would happen if I didn't ask him to forgive a specific sin? Does that sin remain without forgiveness until the day that I die? What happens in eternity? I know enough about Scripture to know nobody gets in heaven with sin because God hates sin, so does that mean I wouldn't be going to heaven?

As a confused teenager, I imagined myself being eternally separated from God because I called a guy in the car next to me an idiot—a sin for which I never asked forgiveness. Do you see where this thought process is going? What if I was eternally separated from God because I died in a car crash after I had angry thoughts about the person driving beside me who just cut me off?

Let's just complicate this a bit more. James 4:17 says that it's a sin to know what you ought to do and not do it. This puts an exponential rate on the thought process of needing to have every sin be forgiven. Not only does sin include the things we did that we shouldn't have done, but it includes good things that we knew to do and didn't.

Seriously, if you believe you have to confess every sin so they can all be forgiven, you better just live a perfect life. But I'll warn you right now, trying to keep up with perfection will make you have a nervous breakdown.

Forever Is a Long Time

Let's review. What is the one thing that makes God mad?

Sin.

That's good news.

Why?

Because our sin was dealt with on the cross in totality. In Jesus, you were forgiven. It's finished.

Acts 10:43 says, "He is the one all the prophets testified about, saying that everyone who believes in him will have their sins forgiven through his name." Does it say just some of their sins would be forgiven? Nope. All of them. In fact, there's a lot more scriptural proof that all of your sins were taken care of on the cross:

> We are here to proclaim that through this man Jesus there is forgiveness for your sins. (Acts 13:38)

> He is so rich in kindness and grace that he purchased our freedom with the blood of his Son and forgave our sins. (Eph. 1:7)

> Instead, be kind to each other, tenderhearted, forgiving one another, just as God through Christ has forgiven you. (Eph. 4:32)

> For he has rescued us from the kingdom of darkness and transferred us into the Kingdom of

his dear Son, who purchased our freedom and forgave our sins. (Col. 1:13–14)

I am writing to you who are God's children because your sins have been forgiven through Jesus. (1 John 2:12)

Seeing their faith, Jesus said to the man, "Young man, your sins are forgiven." (Luke 5:20)

What's my point here? God accepts you. Now, accept yourself. I know many Christians struggle with the guilt of their sins hanging over their lives. They know, intellectually, they've been forgiven, but the truth of that has not been received at the emotional level.

> God accepts you. Now, accept yourself.

One Spot in Time

If Jesus were to come sit next to you right now, put His arm around you, take His other hand and turn your face toward Him, hold your cheek, and look at you eyeball to eyeball; and if He were to list every sin you ever committed and every skeleton in your closet and every sin you're going to commit that you don't know about; and if He were to list your present plan for discipleship and whatever that includes or doesn't include, or your lack of discipleship, and all of your hidden agendas and schemes of your lifetime; let me tell you something . . . Even in that moment, you would feel His forgiveness. You would feel His mercy.

Listen, He's not mad at you. Yet, we believe that, don't we? Sometimes it's the Devil or religion trying to convince us our repeated sinning must wear on Jesus' patience. But the truth is, no, it doesn't.

You cannot out-sin the grace of God. If you could, you wouldn't be able to be saved. Romans 5:20 says, "God's law was given so that all people could see how sinful they were. But as people sinned more and more, God's wonderful grace became more abundant." That's the whole point of the law. The law was like an object lesson illustrating how sinful we are by nature. But even now as people sin more and more, God's wonderful kindness becomes even more abundant.

The Thou-Shalts and the Thou-Shalt-Nots

Some of you may argue that many respectable teachers and preachers teach about Scriptures that command us to do/not do certain acts. I admit, I have taught some thou-shalts and thou-shalt-nots. So why would anyone teach those things if they didn't apply to the lives of Christians?

Let me make an important distinction here. I'm not saying that a Christian's life should be without good works. There's a place for good works in the believer's life. I'm saying that your good works have no bearing whatsoever on whether or not God accepts you. Salvation is a free gift—no strings attached. You cannot do anything to earn it. You cannot do anything to keep it. It was given to you.

The commandments of Scripture are not a doorway to victory. There is only one doorway to victory. It is the person of Jesus Christ. Period. So when we're talking about works the Bible teaches should be a part of a Christian's life, the important question to ask is, "What's my motivation?"

You can choose between two lenses to view the commandments in Scripture. Lens number one is a legalistic lens—a law-oriented way where you believe you follow the commandments because you *have* to. This is a negative way to look at the Scriptures, as if all of the commands are things we ought to do that hang over our heads to remind us of how far we are from being fully accepted by God. Ultimately, this creates in us a compelling sense of guilt.

The legalist reads John 14:15, as "Keep My commandments to show Me that you love Me." But that's not what the verse says: "If you love me, obey my commandments." Not to show Me that you love Me. Not so that I love you. It's *because of* love that we keep the commandments of God.

On the other hand, you can view the commandments through the lens of grace. The grace-oriented lens does not see these commandments as obligations; it sees these commandments as opportunities for the life of Jesus Christ to be revealed through us. In other words, what's in me can come out of me and be a testimony to all those that are around me.[12]

Welcome to Grace Land

Naturally, this discussion leads to the question, *Are you teaching that all Christians can go and do whatever they want to do?*

Absolutely not. Yes, you can do anything you want—in grace. But the grace of God teaches Christians to deny ungodliness and live holy lives. It's not so you can earn the favor of God—the favor of God is already in you.

A legalist is afraid of this concept. The legalist is afraid of this kind of grace because he has never experienced the freedom to commit the kinds of sins he knows in his heart he's capable of committing given the chance. If he's never been given that freedom, he thinks this kind of freedom is scary, so scary it may even scare him to death.

Sound familiar? If so, you might be a legalist, but let me tell you something—you're not alone. This is an age-old dilemma. Even Paul had to deal with it in Bible times: "Well then, should we keep on sinning so that God can show us more and more of his wonderful grace?" (Rom. 6:1).

Why would somebody ask that? Because Paul had been teaching about this amazing grace from God, and as the people began to understand God's amazing grace, they asked this question. They knew that His grace would provide more and more kindness and forgiveness, but Paul's answer is clear, "Of course not!" (v. 2). In the Greek, it means "let it never be."

He continues in the same verse, "Since we have died to sin, how can we continue to live in it?" Did you see that? We have died to sin. Died. How then could we continue living in it? Maybe you've forgotten that when you became a Christian, *you died with Him*. This sin thing is dead.

So What?

One of my college friends (we'll call him Joe) was a real intellectual. While he tried to decide whether or not to follow God, he took the time to sit down and thoroughly discuss all of his doubts and questions with one of our professors and me. I remember the day he admitted he wanted to believe the Bible and trust Jesus, but the fear of failure was holding him back. He was concerned that after he committed his life to God, he'd fail and let God down.

Our professor's response was unforgettable. He shrugged and asked, "So what?" He went on to explain that Joe (and all who commit to God) was going to fail, and, more than likely, he was going to fail big time; but that wouldn't make any difference in his standing with God.

God doesn't deposit forgiveness into an account with our names on it so we can make forgiveness withdrawals when we need them. If He did, we'd all be in overdraft in a short period of time. Instead, He emptied the entire forgiveness bank on us. He cancelled the record: "He has removed our sins as far from us as the east is from the west" (Ps. 103:12). Why did the author of Psalms describe it this way? Because no one can ever go east and get west.

That's what He does with our sins. Anytime we fail and ask forgiveness, the record is cancelled again. God doesn't remember it.

If God refused to condemn you because your works were rotten, He won't flunk you because your faith isn't perfect.

Sin Time Line

Think of your life up to this point as a time line. Every sin you've committed marks a step forward in your time line. Scanning over those sins, which would you choose as the worst sin of your life? Think about the details of that sin. Do you remember any of the specifics? The sights? The smells? The feeling in your gut? The looks from the people around you when they found out?

Now, envision Jesus on a cross bleeding, weeping, crown-of-thorns-pierced head hanging in agony. Picture Him looking into your eyes and saying in a calm, passion-filled voice, "I love you, My child. I know about your worst sins, and I forgive you. That's why I'm here on this cross. Now, forgive yourself, and let's never mention this again."

That moment happened two thousand years ago. It happened before you were born. It happened before you committed that terrible sin you're remembering. It's taken care of. It was cancelled from your record. All you have to do is choose to believe and commit your life to Jesus.

And once you do that, refuse to feel guilty about those sins again. God made it clear in the Bible that those sins have been removed. Now it's time to start living like you believe it. It's truth. It's done. It's taken care of. Let go of the past.

Guilt will not make you a better person. It will not deepen your walk with God. And it certainly won't earn you more favor in God's eyes. God provided forgiveness so you could walk away from that guilt. He never intended for you to drag it around with you.

Let it go. Leave it behind. And don't let anyone take you back to that guilt and talk you into picking it back up again. Cancel it from your memory. It's forgiven. God is and always will be sufficient.

Study Questions

1. What are three things you blame yourself for doing wrong when you go down "Accusation Road"?

2. What obstacles are you facing that prevent you from believing Jesus' death on the cross can take care of *all* of your sins?

3. What's the difference between following God's commandments because you *have to* and because you *get to*?

Chapter Ten

The Religion of Works

Sometimes we get so caught up in "doing good" and "acting right" to score points with God that we miss what He really wants from us, which is a relationship. If we are only going through the motions out of guilt or duty, we are not free to love God. He wants our hearts first! God loves us unconditionally, so once we try to "earn" that love, we are falling into "religion." Jesus came to free us from it so we can have a true relationship with the Father. As we develop that relationship, we allow God to work in us and through us to "do what is right." For those of you who are struggling to be good, relax and let God love you where you're at. When we concentrate on duty/ rules, we replace relationship with religion.

—D. [Excerpted from www.jesushates
religion.com message board]

Religion is a path paved with deeds: good deeds, better deeds, and best deeds. And whether you've journeyed down one of the four paths we've discussed so far (self, legalism, inferiority, or guilt), or whether you're on the path I'm about to describe (works), you're about to hit a crossroads. It's time to recognize the directional impairment our paths have been following and stop living by bad directions. Bad directions will always take you down a path of trying to please God instead of a path of trusting God.

Jesus, who is our true north, described His mission as coming to seek and save the lost (Luke 19:10). He came and released the chains of bondage. He stood against the burden of religion, and He found a world that didn't appreciate His message. But that didn't shake His goals. Jesus was about transforming and renewing people's minds to who He is. He never intended to come to earth with the purpose of putting up a bunch of "do not enter" signs. He was about freedom.

It's always been your choice to follow or reject God. Always. You are the only one who can choose the path your life is going to follow. You can choose one of these religion paths—self, legalism, inferiority, guilt, or works—or you can take the path God forged for you—salvation as a free gift.

What's Wrong with Good Works?

The religion of works is the pursuit of stacking up good deeds. Basically, it's putting a dependency on righteous acts, which in turn focuses on self-righteousness. Already, I'm sure you can see the red flags that come with depending on good works. It's once again shifting the focus from God and His offer of salvation as a gift, and shifting it onto our own accomplishments and effort. Yet we continue to justify our trust in good works because we believe it will lead to God saying, "I accept you." But it doesn't work that way.

Look at the book of Galatians, a New Testament book of the Bible, and what Paul has to say to the church of Galatia: "How foolish can you be? After starting your Christian lives in the Spirit, why are you now trying to become perfect by your own human effort?" (3:3). Sound familiar? Again, God is making it clear that your human effort has nothing to do with your salvation.

This would be a good time to read all of Galatians. It was originally written as a letter to a group of people. If you received a letter in the mail or a personal e-mail from a friend, you wouldn't break it down into paragraphs and read it over the course of a month or even a week. More than likely, you'd sit down and read it from beginning to end. If you didn't, it's likely you'd forget important parts toward the beginning, and you may have trouble making connections from one place to the next. The same is true of Galatians and all of the letters from Romans to Jude; each is meant to be read all at once.

Works Deconstructed

The religion of works naturally appeals to our flesh. Remember, the flesh wants to be in control and make sure God is nowhere near the steering wheel of our lives. So when we focus on what we're doing, we're taking away from what God already did and putting ourselves back in the driver's seats.

Why is this so enticing? Because we've bought into the lie of works: victorious living is avoiding the wrong actions and doing the right actions.

If you think victorious living in your Christian life is avoiding bad things and doing good things, you've been deceived. Here's how it usually plays out: People begin to believe that they're going to gain spiritual mileage by revving up their religious RPMs. They believe the essence of Christian living is finding out what the Bible says and then striving to do it. For those of you, like me, who live by lists, this is especially alluring.

I live by my calendar. I'm an Outlook disciple and Franklin Covey follower. If I get sidetracked in my

ADD and do something that isn't on my list, I write it in just so I can check it off. When I was a child, I looked forward to filling out my offering envelope because on the back they had a scorecard of good works to check off each week:

Did you read your Bible every day? Check.

Did you pray? Check.

Did you give your tithe? Check.

It was like filling out my own report card—I always knew I was going to get an A. It wasn't until I was older and had years of experience working in the churches that I realized no one ever looked at those cards, let alone graded them. The scores weren't tallied and entered in a database. Yet, I found such great satisfaction in checking off each item and patting myself on the back for a job well done. I believed I was victorious because I accomplished the right things, and I avoided the wrong things each week.

As a teenager, I took this religion to a whole new level. I remember getting home from church each Sunday, eating lunch, and then jumping back in the car to go to youth choir at four. After that I'd go to discipleship training, and finally, I'd end my day attending the Sunday evening service. My dad thought this was ridiculous and would always ask me where I was going. When I tried to explain my intentions, he'd counter with, "No, son, that's for people who missed church this morning. You're covered already." I used to think he was just *so unspiritual*, but now I realize how wise he was. He knew my priorities were all out of whack. I was putting my faith in my oh-so-spiritual schedule instead of putting my faith in God.

The same believer who knows he didn't come to Jesus by earning his salvation by good works can still easily end up in the religion of works where he believes that *after* he's saved, his whole life should revolve around doing good for God. Have you heard the song, "Mary had a little lamb, it used to be a sheep. Then it joined a local church, and it died from lack of sleep"?[13] I was on a fast track to the same demise. I was using the Bible to get instructions concerning what God expects of me once I'm saved. I believed the efforts of an unsaved person would yield no spiritual progress, but the efforts of a saved man would guarantee me spiritual results.

I was sincere in my attempts to advance spiritually—sincerely wrong. Self-effort, even for a Christian, is wood, hay, and straw: it will burn to nothing. It's not going to last forever, and it will only yield frustration.

But Why?

So if works are clearly not the path God intended for us to follow, why are we so easily duped into believing this? There are a couple of answers to that. First of all, it seems logical that God expects our best.[14] That just resonates between the ears for all of us. We don't even know of another way.

Throughout my life, I've talked to several Muslims about Christ. The one common argument they always try to throw back at me is, "You try to follow Christ by keeping the Bible, and we try to follow Allah by keeping the Koran." Many believers would shrug and agree, "Well, that's true," but I'm telling you it's not!

Sure, if we're talking about religion, then, yes, that statement's true. But I'm talking about biblical Christianity. Christianity is a literal union with the person of Jesus Christ where by faith you trust Jesus to do in you what you cannot do yourself. It's not about reading this Book and trying to follow Jesus by doing what the Bible says. It's a union with Jesus.

If we don't know the difference between following a book of rules and having a union with Jesus, we're bound to believe that line of thinking is logical. Plus, it feeds our ego and our senses of accomplishment. Who doesn't want to get to his deathbed and be able to think about all the great things he's done for God?

Surely there's an extra big blessing waiting in heaven to reward each person who has committed their lives to doing good things for God, right? But that's where we get tripped up. Once we adopt this way of thinking, we're back in self-effort. And the ultimate difference lies in *fulfillment for what you did versus contentment in who you are.* It's a big difference. Don't move on until you understand that.

You can be fulfilled without being content. When people love you, when you have a large crowd follow-ing you, when you grow a big church or ministry, or when you're showered with appreciation for the hard work you've done, you may feel fulfilled.

> Self-effort can gratify, but it can never satisfy.

Those things are certainly fulfilling, but they don't bring contentment. Self-effort can gratify, but it can never satisfy.

I.O.U.

Sure, guilt will always be an effective motivator. I mean, who wants to argue that we don't owe God everything? But what people don't understand is that grace can never be repaid. Never.

Quit trying. It's a futile battle. Grace has no price, not because it's worthless, but because it's priceless. It's beyond the mentality of "you scratch my back, I'll scratch yours," so stop trying to figure out how you can repay God. You can't.

I know we all desire to gain God's acceptance and what's better than total acceptance from God? But if God's acceptance of you is already unconditional and perfect, how could you improve on that? Honestly, you have nothing to contribute to this equation. Nothing you can do can cause God to love you any more than He already does. Besides, if doing is the measuring, how will you know when you've done enough?

But, That's the Law

Just because it's the law, doesn't mean it's the answer. Jesus tells us to never return to the rules. He told us to come to Him alone. He wants to be in a relationship with us. This Christian journey doesn't revolve around being good, but it's an age-old myth to think so.

Galatians deals with this issue at great length. Start with Galatians 3:1–3:

> Oh, foolish Galatians! Who has cast an evil spell on you? For the meaning of Jesus Christ's death was made as clear to you as if you had

seen a picture of his death on the cross. Let me ask you this one question: Did you receive the Holy Spirit by obeying the law of Moses? Of course not! You received the Spirit because you believed the message you heard about Christ. How foolish can you be? After starting your Christian lives in the Spirit, why are you now trying to become perfect by your own human effort?

What's wrong with the religion of works? Jesus did not come to help us do right. He came to help us know Him. And for us to know Him, He came to deliver us from the law. The law never died. Our relationship to the law died. The law is still around. In relationship to the law, we as Christians know we aren't supposed to break it, but are we supposed to keep it?

The answer is simple. Can a dead man follow rules? No, of course not. He's dead. He can't do anything. Our relationship to the law died when Christ died on the cross for our sins. Died. Dead. It's a goner. No more possible is it for my dead relatives to come knocking on my door and join me for dinner than it is for us to keep the law.

What's Your Function?

There are two things the law is good for.[15] Number one, it stimulates sin.

What?

Check out 1 Corinthians 15:56, "For sin is the sting that results in death, and the law gives sin its power." That's not the only verse either. Romans 7:5 says, "When we were controlled by our old nature, sinful desires were at work within us, and the law aroused these evil desires that produced a harvest of sinful deeds, resulting in death."

The second function of the law is administering death and condemnation. Look at 2 Corinthians 3:7, "The old way, with laws etched in stone, led to death." In other words, when you're obsessed with rules, it's idolatry. The rules are the idol.

I've done a lot of marriage counseling, and it never ceases to amaze me the questions I am asked. One I hear more often than I'd like to admit is "Do I have to kiss my wife?" It's times like those that I wish I had the power to freeze time, pull the bride-to-be aside, and plead with her to run!

I don't need the rules of marriage to tell me to kiss my wife. I love my wife, and because I love my wife, I want to kiss her. I might even love her more than she loves me because I want to kiss her more than she wants to kiss me.

But don't you see? That's the problem with the religion of works. The law can tell us what to do, but it will never give us the ability to fulfill it. Jesus is the one who does that. Satan knows the best way to defeat those who come to Christ is make them believe that obeying the law is the pathway to victory; but the harder you try, the more certain you are to fail.

Works are just the litmus tests: James 2:14 says, "What good is it, dear brothers and sisters, if you say you have faith but don't show it by your actions? Can that kind of faith save anyone?" Here, James is saying if you really love God and God really loves you and lives in you, works are going to play out in your life—you won't be able to hide them. Consequently, if those actions aren't playing out in your life, then you've got an issue.

Simmer Down

In grace, God does it all. We simply receive from Him. We're grateful beneficiaries—grateful for what God has done in our lives. We're not providers for ourselves or for anyone else. Self-effort is a barrier to rest; yet the Christian culture today opposes rest. Today we go on vacation with cell phones, personal organizers, and laptops, and we believe that resting in God is lazy and negligent. But this is not true.

True resting is trusting Jesus as your life source. It's depending on Him to empower your actions with His strength and direction. It's choosing a new mind-set— one unobstructed by culture's opinions of how you should conduct life:

> Then Jesus said, "Come to me, all of you who are weary and carry heavy burdens, and I will give you rest. Take my yoke upon you. Let me teach you, because I am humble and gentle at heart, and you will find rest for your souls. For my yoke is easy to bear, and the burden I give you is light." (Matt. 11:28–30)

Not only do I prepare for a lot of marriage counseling and retreats, I also perform a lot of funerals. For many years, I'd use Hebrews 4:10, "For all who have entered into God's rest have rested from their labors, just as God did after creating the world" as a source of comfort for the families of the deceased. But one day I was early to a funeral, so I was reading through that passage of Scripture, and I saw that in the very next verse it says, "So let us do our best to enter that rest." God's not promoting suicide here. He's leading by example and demonstrating His rest leads to greatness. It's God doing something in you while you're alive on this side of eternity.

Have you ever been in a hospital and seen somebody on a respirator? Horrible. Absolutely one of the most desperate sights you can see. But if the respirator is going to do its job, that person has to relax. If she isn't unconscious, she'd probably rip out the very instrument that's keeping her alive by breathing for her.

The Holy Spirit in the Greek is the word *nooma*. It means "breath." Isn't that an amazing illustration of how God wants to breathe for you? When He breathes for you, true rest comes. At that point, Jesus really is your life. The Holy Spirit can flow through you as naturally as breath flows in and out of your lungs. Jesus can move in you and minister through you.

The Christian life can be easy. You've just got to let God do it. You're free from the law and attempting to do things for God. Instead, grace says that God does something for you. Church attendance, Bible reading, prayer, giving, witnessing are all good things; but they should be the result of intimacy.

Study Questions

1. What are some good works you've been guilty of believing would earn you favor with God?

2. What's the difference between feeling fulfilled for what you've done versus being content in who you are?

3. How can knowing good works has nothing to do with your salvation change your day-to-day life?

4. What are two functions of the law and how do they impact or influence our lives?

Chapter Eleven

The Role of Good Works

Well, so far from what I understand, religion is more law than relationship. Jesus hates religion, but what about God? Does He? The Jewish have been very religious and have followed the law to the T. They were more about religion than relationship from what I have heard and understand. Religion and relationship is more of a balance than one overpowering the other. God withholds the religion, and Jesus withholds the relationship. Of course, God wants a relationship, but I don't think He is the one to go to if you want to look for good relationship tips. When reading the Bible, Jesus seems to be about relationships with people. He was always talking to people, no matter if it were His followers or if it were the taxpayers. God is more of the fatherly type to us. He

*seems to be the law keeper or the iron fist. So we need
to see both sides and where they come from.*
　　　　　　—O. C. [Excerpted from www.jesushates
　　　　　　　　　　religion.com message board]

If you've gotten this far in the book and believe that there's no place for good works in the life of a believer, then I have failed you as an author. Never once in this book have you read the statement that good works should be eliminated from a Christian's life. What you have read is that good works have nothing to do with a Christian's salvation. Nothing. If any part of your salvation is based on works then it is not biblical. You have also read that good works have nothing to do with earning favor from God. Because of Jesus, God accepts you completely and totally as you are right now.

But neither of those statements implies that good works are to be void from a Christian's life. As I'm sure you're very familiar, the Bible is full of "dos" and "don'ts." Whether it's Old Testament or New Testament, there are plenty of verses that describe what a Christian should and shouldn't do. So how does all of this fit in the life of a Christian?

When I was working with my staff on the construction plans for our new church building, I had a set of blueprints to follow for determining which adjustments needed to be made. To an architect, this is a sufficient tool for visualizing the finished product; but for me, it was clear as mud. When walls started being erected and rooms started being sheet rocked, I started realizing how different my vision of the building was from the architect's. What I needed was a built-to-scale model. If I could have put my hands on something tangible, then I could have clearly followed what the architect was planning. Without that model, the finished product was a pretty big mystery to me.

God understands the value of a real-life model, so He sent His Son Jesus to show us what a life surrendered to the Father should look like. Jesus' example is what sets the Old Testament apart from the New Testament. The Old Testament is basically a 2-D model, like the blueprints, with lists and lists of thou-shalts and thou-shalt-nots. All of the Old Testament is looking forward to the coming of Jesus. But the New Testament details Jesus' life on this planet and all of the experiences and difficulties that He dealt with. He was a six-foot, living, breathing, 4-D model that we could turn to for all of our answers: "For God knew his people in advance, and he chose them to become like his Son, so that his Son would be the firstborn among many brothers and sisters" (Rom. 8:29).

It's been God's plan from the beginning for you and me to be like Jesus. I'm not talking about dressing like

Him (which would be weird), or trying to associate with the same type of people He associated with. I'm talking about focusing on being internally conformed to the image of Jesus. It's impossible to know what Jesus would do in every given situation, but it *is* possible for Jesus to live His life in and through us so that we can love like Him, be patient like Him, exercise self-control like Him, be kind and gentle like Him.

It is not about human effort. It is about God and all He has already provided. God has given us the model, the tools, and the means to the end—now go use them.

Remember, the end goal here is not a better, more cleaned up, more spiritual version of yourself. The goal here is a reflection of Jesus. It's not something you can manufacture; it's produced through you. When you manufacture a product, you try, you produce, then you work harder to make a better product. But you can't manufacture Jesus—He is the only one who can make that happen.

> The end goal here is not a better, more cleaned up, more spiritual version of yourself. The goal here is a reflection of Jesus.

Back to Habitation

Earlier I mentioned how the Christian life is not about imitation; it's about habitation. Look at John 15:5, "'Yes, I am the vine; you are the branches. Those who remain in me, and I in them, will produce much fruit. For apart from me you can do nothing.'" Jesus is saying our sole responsibility is to abide. That's it. Just abide. Apart from Jesus you can't do anything, so you've got to abide in Him.

The original word used for *abide* in the Greek carries the meaning of moving in or living with someone. It's a relational word. It means that you stay close—so close that you experience uninterrupted fellowship. It's more than just an occasional exchange with an acquaintance. God wants all of you all of the time. When you give all to Him, He can do great things through you.

When you focus on abiding rather than becoming, you will see good works happen in your life that you didn't even think you were capable of. These works are the direct result of your habitation in Jesus. You can't manufacture them. Jesus is the only One who can produce this life in you; your responsibility is to abide.

Look at the preceding four verses in John 15:

"I am the true grapevine, and my Father is the gardener. He cuts off every branch of mine that doesn't produce fruit, and he prunes the branches that do bear fruit so they will produce even more. You have already been pruned and purified by the message I have given you. Remain in me, and I will remain in you. For a branch cannot produce fruit if it is severed from the vine, and you cannot be fruitful unless you remain in me."

Nothing is possible—not being patient, not overcoming temptation—without God. God doesn't even promise that He'll make *us* capable. He says He will *do it in us*.

> God doesn't even promise that He'll make *us* capable. He says He will *do it in us*.

Change Your Thinking

In order to fully grasp this, it's important to recognize the lies that are affecting your actions and beginning to change your thinking. Our Enemy, the Devil, will attempt to divert our attention primarily in three areas. He knows that if he can divert our attention in one or more of these areas that he can throw us off target regularly. He wants to divert our attention off of a relationship with Jesus and direct it toward religion.

Merely believing in God didn't make lasting changes in my life. But when I began a relationship with Him, the change occurred. If you're thinking religiously, you believe God is somewhere out there, and your goal in life is trying to please Him. You think God is some guy up there in the distance that will give you a gold star if you behave properly. Most people hope heaven's not really like that. God sent His Son to earth to bridge the gap between God and man, not to make it wider.

On the other hand, if you're thinking relationally, your thoughts are focused on staying close to God. There's an intimacy that comes with relationship, and there's an inherent desire to be together. A close relationship is something you can't easily cast aside.

The Enemy also attempts to take our attention and focus off of association with Jesus and direct it toward imitation instead. If he can get us focused on "trying to do things like Jesus did," rather than enjoying life in relationship with Him, he can trap us. You can't imitate Jesus any more successfully than you can imitate Lebron James on the basketball court; your ability to do so would be an obvious shortfall. Instead your association with Jesus, being found in Christ, needs to be the focus. The branch doesn't ever try to imitate the vine; it simply abides.

Last, the Enemy would also have you think that if you work and work and work at it, then eventually you will be able to beat temptation. However, Jesus wants you to confess that you can't beat it and trust that He can through you. Stop saying, "I can't," and start saying, "I can't, but He can through me." Too many times I hear people express their frustrations in the form of "I can'ts": "I can't be patient with her one more day," "I can't deal with this temptation at the office anymore," "I can't control myself when I'm on the Internet," etc. It's time to wave the white flag and say, "Jesus says I can." No matter how deep you are into sin, Jesus has promised He is still willing to relate to you if you will relate to Him. Think of it this way: "I can't, but I surrender."

Baby Models

It's easy to see this idea demonstrated in the life of a person who has just experienced salvation. The Bible compares people who are newly saved to babies (1 Pet. 2:2)—they need to learn, grow, develop, etc. At the baby stage there are very few things they know besides the facts that they are now forgiven and God loves them. These two truths in and of themselves are a lot to wrap their brains around. Baby Christians aren't necessarily immediately trying to change their lifestyle; their focus is on relationship. But lo and behold, the fruit (the good works) is there too.

Later down the line when they've heard a variety of teachings, been caught up in the lie of good works, and begin to rely on themselves rather than God. They get away from this natural fruit being a part of their lives.

If you've drifted away from this natural inclination to do good works as a result of your salvation, go back to that complete reliance on God. Abide in Him. Remember, you're forgiven. You didn't do anything to earn your salvation or God's favor. Develop a relationship with God, and the good works will be a natural outgrowth of your habitation.

I love seeing someone who has been a Christian for a long time come to a point where they wave the white flag and admit, "I can't, but God can through me." At that moment, God rolls up His sleeves and provides something so new and fresh the person feels as if they became a Christian all over again.

It doesn't matter how long you've been a Christian. Whether it's been a few hours or your entire life, you can't successfully imitate Christ. It's time to stop trying and start abiding.

Study Questions

1. What are some common excuses people use to avoid following Jesus' example?

2. What are some areas in your life that are overwhelming you because you are trying to do it on your own?

3. Who are some Christ followers that you believe are producing good works? Why do you think it is happening in them?

Chapter Twelve

Pass It On

If Jesus came down right now, He would actu-
ally be very disappointed in the majority of all so-
called Christians. If Jesus said to love all people,
then why is it that you always see a group of people
protesting about one thing or the other? And if you
take any notice, the majority of the time it is the
self-proclaimed Christians saying that it is "against
God's will" Is everything against God? Sounds to me
like you're just afraid of what you don't understand,
which is in our human nature. But the fact of the
matter is that if God said to love all, then why won't
you do just that? Why won't you come out of your
comfort zone and open your mind and accept people
as they are and treat them as the children of God
instead of treating them like sinners? Because I'm
sure that your mothers all taught you the rule that

says to treat others as you would wish to be treated.
And where do you suppose that one came from, huh?
—C. [Excerpted from www.jesushates
religion.com message board]

G od has created you with specific gifts, opportunities, and skills. Once you begin abiding in
Christ, you will see how God can put those
skills into action and use you to make a difference in
this world. You were created with a purpose, but God
won't force you to do anything you don't want to do.
He's waiting for you to abide and allow Him to work
through you.

The Bible compares the church to the body of Christ.
Just as a human body has many parts with many functions, the body of Christ has many people with many
different skill sets. The beauty of God's creation is He
didn't create a church full of eyeballs. Each person has
a different function, and when that function is incor-
porated into the body of
Christ, it complements
the other members. Plus,
the body functions best
when it becomes a sum of
its parts.

> The beauty of God's creation is He didn't create a church full of eyeballs.

Stick with Us

Just like the body cannot properly function if it is just one big hand, you, as a Christian, will not function properly if you isolate yourself. Being independent is trendy, and it sounds right: "You take care of yours, and I'll take care of mine." But independence ultimately leads to isolation, and isolation leads to self-centeredness.

Isn't it funny how people look up to leaders who are labeled independent, yet when we change the label to self-centered, the people's opinion drastically changes? The church is guilty of the same thing. If the church doesn't recognize that it functions best as a sum of its parts, then people will branch off and isolate themselves. It's dangerous to try to do the Christian walk alone. A majority of the people whose lives are a bad testimony of Christianity are people who have disconnected from the vine and tried living as self-sufficient branches—it's just not natural, and it doesn't work.

The good news is that the cycle of self-centeredness can be broken. The best way to break that cycle is to look back to the Bible. Galatians 6:2 says, "Carry each other's burdens, and in this way you will fulfill the law of Christ" (NIV). Now, before you get all huffy and try to convince me this is asking too much, let me break this verse down a little more for you. The word *burden* implies something that is so big another person can't carry it on his own. This concept goes back to Old Testament law in Deuteronomy 22:4 where the Bible says, "If you see your brother's donkey or his ox fallen on the road, do not ignore it" (NIV). I call this a "no duh!" law—if you see a guy who needs help, help him. Easier said than done, though, and somewhere in history we have lost sight of how to do this.

If you continue reading in Galatians 6:5, it says, "Each one should carry his own load" (NIV). On the surface that seems contradictory. If each person should carry his own load, why would we need to bother with carrying other people's burdens? They should take care of it themselves, right? But this is where knowing the origins of biblical words helps. A load is different from a burden, like a large boulder is different from a small pack. When the Bible encourages us to carry each other's burdens, what seems like a large boulder to the person carrying it, is like a small pack for us to pick up.

Picture a toddler trying to carry a small bag of groceries from the car to the kitchen. To that toddler, the bag is a cumbersome burden half the size of his little body. An action as simple as taking one step up into the kitchen is now almost impossible without the use of his hands and arms for balance. In addition, hoisting that bag of groceries on top of anything higher than knee-level is a huge feat. But if you were to come along and add the bag to your own load, it would seem almost inconsequential.

God is not asking you to take other people's big boulders and add them to your own. He's asking you to do what you can, knowing full well what you can do is well within your abilities and will prove to be little extra personal burden.

If this is all God is asking, what keeps us from obeying? Why don't we reach out and help when we see someone in need? Some will argue they can't be bothered to help because they're on their way to something else. Listen, if we're too busy to help others, we're too busy.

People who don't help because they don't think they are strong enough or have the right talents are also missing the point. If I drive by someone on the side of the road who has driven into a ditch, I know that by myself I cannot be much help. But if I stop to help, I can direct traffic, while another guy with a 4x4 pulls out the car, and another person comforts the wife of the

> If we're too busy to help others, we're too busy.

driver. As we carry our part of the burden, our neighbor is able to get his life back on track.

See, God is not asking us to be stronger or different than who we are. He's given each of us the right amount of strength and skills to help when we can. As I mentioned earlier in the book, I am half Egyptian. I have a great love and burden for that country. Because of this, our church has made many mission trips there. Taxi drivers in Egypt are a great example of this principle. When a person gets in a cab and gives the driver the destination, he'll shrug, "Yeah, yeah," and start driving. A few minutes into the trip he stops and asks for directions, but he doesn't just ask one person; he stops and asks multiple people. The cabbie knows that even if the person he asks doesn't know the answer, he will try to help out anyway and give his best guess as to the correct directions. The driver then takes the average of everyone's directions, and, eventually, he makes it to his destination.

How many of us would use the excuse, "Well, I'm not sure I would be any help, so I'll just stay out of your way"? God isn't asking us to repair a carburetor or do advanced math. He's just asking us to help lighten the collective load. We all can do that, and the more people, the lighter everyone's share.

The Law of Love

There's something incredible that happens when we stop to help others. Paul describes it as fulfilling the law (Gal. 6:2).

Whoa! You told me the law produces sin and leads to death. I don't remember Jesus giving me a new ten commandments.

The law Paul is addressing in Galatians is the law of Christ or the law of love. In Matthew 22, a teacher of the law (Old Testament) comes to test Jesus, and he asks Jesus what the most important law is.

Jesus knows the answer. It's elementary rabbinic stuff. Easy. But, remember, this was a test to trick Jesus. At the time there were big debates about laws and which ones were important to keep and which were not. It was a slippery slope to try and answer that question, but Jesus handled it with ease, "'Love the LORD your God with all your heart and with all your soul and with all your mind'" (v. 37).

At this point, the teacher of the law may have figured he had trapped Jesus because Jesus just gave some vague answer about loving God. He knows he could fire back with, "Does that mean as long as we love God, we can disobey all the other laws?"

But before he gets a chance to counter, Jesus continues, "'and the second is like it: Love your neighbor as yourself'" (v. 39).

Silence.

Jesus basically tells him that if you really love God, then you won't need to be told what to do. You won't need to debate what's important and what's not. All you'll have to consider is how you want to be treated and then do that for others. That's the law of Christ—loving others as much as yourself.

When people follow the law as a means of gaining favor with God, their motivation is to boost their own self-love. Abiding by the rules makes them feel better about who they are. But Paul points out that this kind of self-love is actually empty: "If you think you are too important to help someone, you are only fooling yourself. You are not that important" (Gal. 6:3).

Whoa! Did he really say that and mean it?

Absolutely.

Paul isn't saying we are nothing to God, nor is he telling us to look at ourselves as nothing. We should take pride and have a good opinion of ourselves, but when our opinion gets so big we think we're better than we really are (or we can't be bothered to help others), we are deceived.

In Philippians 2:3–8, the same warning exists; it's just worded a little differently:

> Don't be selfish; don't try to impress others. Be humble, thinking of others as better than yourselves. Don't look out only for your own interests, but take an interest in others, too. You must have the same attitude that Christ Jesus had. Though he was God, he did not think of equality with God as something to cling to. Instead, he gave up his divine privileges; he took the humble position of a slave and was born as a human being. When he appeared in human form, he humbled himself in obedience to God and died a criminal's death on a cross.

Remember, Jesus was our model—a living, breathing, ultimate model. Notice that Jesus made Himself nothing, became a servant, and died on the cross. If we are to allow Him to work through us, there is no room for self-centered attitudes. It's our responsibility to serve and allow God to use the gifts He's created within us to help others. It will come naturally when you abide in Him and allow God to work through you.

Invitation List

Another natural outcome of abiding in Christ is a desire to invite others to join the journey. God's ultimate purpose in transforming our lives is so He can reveal Himself in this world through those who abide in Him. This is the ultimate intention of Father God, and, honestly, we find our greatest contentment when we fulfill His divine purpose.

Parents, if you had only one child in whom you found unspeakable delight, wouldn't you naturally want more? The same is true of the Father. He desired and purposed to have a family of human children who are just like His only begotten Son. Christianity sets itself apart from other belief systems because its focus is outward. Empty religions seek to preserve themselves and focus on gathering, but Christianity focuses on pouring itself out in ministry to others.

> Christianity is not just about what happens in you personally; it's about allowing Christ to express His life through you.

As I've said so many times in this book, when you take your dependence off of God and put it on yourself, you're missing the best God has planned for you. But when you're abiding in Jesus and trusting completely in God, your life becomes a living testimony to others of God's love and greatness. Christianity is not just about what happens in you personally; it's about allowing Christ to express His life through you.

Inward versus Outward

I realize that personal fulfillment is a wonderful by-product of Jesus' life within, but God's great goal is to express His life to a needy world. Legalistic religion promises freedom, but it actually causes those who are drawn into its snares to become prisoners of rules. Grace causes the Christian to simply rest in Christ, allowing Him

> Laws will always insist on ministry, but grace inspires it.

to reveal Himself to others in the course of living each day naturally.

Religion makes performance its priority, but grace chooses people as its priority. Grace frees us to take our eyes off ourselves and allows us to invest ourselves in others. It's a freedom that activates ministry motivated by life, not by laws. Laws will always insist on ministry, but grace inspires it.

People or Prospects?

When you've truly abandoned religion and put your full trust in God, His grace changes your way of thinking. No longer are you searching for prospects to add to your religion, now you are looking at a world of people. Just calling somebody a "prospect" instantly depersonalizes that person, which is so far away from how God views His children.

Nowhere in the Bible will you find Jesus referring to people as "prospects," and since He is our ultimate example, when looking for opportunities to share your faith, we are not to take this perspective either. Ultimately, it is a utilitarian viewpoint because people are reduced to resources for building a church. If this viewpoint is carried to an extreme, evangelism with this perspective can become worldly.

A Christian who truly understands the divine grace that salvation is based upon is instinctively hungry to share Jesus' love with others. As I mentioned before, it's a natural fruit of salvation. And, quite honestly, those who are hungry to share God's love are the most effective in reaching others for Christ.

People enter and exit churches because the church-goers within fail to connect with them as people. As soon as a visitor has a notion that he/she is nothing more than a prospect, *sayonara*! Yet there are churches

around the world whose tactic is to promote new con-
verts through the ranks: salvation, membership, volunteer, etc. But this method always fails to connect with
people.

God loves people. In fact, the Bible says He loves us
so much His thoughts can't be numbered:

> How precious to me are your thoughts, O
> God! How vast is the sum of them! Were I to
> count them, they would outnumber the grains
> of sand. (Ps. 139:17–18 NIV)

God loves us as individuals, and when that love lives
in us, we will love people as individuals.

Joy or Job?

When you think of sharing God's love with others,
does it weigh heavy on you like that sick feeling in your
stomach on Sunday night when you know the week-
end's over and it's time to go back to work the next day?
If so, you've shifted out of God's grace and drifted back
into religion where your works are motivated by gaining something for yourself. Sharing God's love should
be a joy.

Evangelism, which is sharing God with others, in
the New Testament was modeled for us as spontaneous

expressions of Christ. It wasn't just a program the church created with a three-step plan to sharing your faith; it was a way of life. A Christian who didn't evangelize would've been like a farmer who didn't plant or a soldier who didn't fight. The New Testament church didn't have to be motivated to share God's love—they couldn't be stopped: "Peter and John replied, 'Judge for yourselves whether it is right in God's sight to obey you rather than God. For we cannot help speaking about what we have seen and heard'" (Acts 4:19–20 NIV).

When people are consumed with joy, they can't be stopped. God's grace fans the flame of a Christian's desire to witness, and it naturally produces a life filled with joy that must be shared with others. God's grace ignites compassion toward the lost and motivates Christians to naturally witness about that grace to others. Grace-based evangelism is nothing less than an excitement about Jesus that is contagious to others.

Person or Plan?

Knowing true grace, a grace that is only found in the person of Jesus Christ, compels Christians to share that person, Jesus, with those around them. That's ultimately what evangelism is really all about—introducing people to Jesus Christ. The Bible, from Genesis to the maps in the back, is about a love affair between the person of God and the people He creates. So when we share the Good News, we are simply saying, "There is a real God, and He really loves you."

Religion will hand you a three-step plan detailing how to share God's love with others. It's intimidating, daunting, and disconnected from God's ultimate desire. He wants sharing your testimony to be a natural outpouring from the joy and grace you experience while following Him. He doesn't want to burden you with a list that prompts your words.

The most effective evangelism leaves a person with more than just knowledge that he/she is a Christian; it leaves that person in love with a person named Jesus. New Christians who understand they have entered into an eternal relationship with the living Christ are assured of their salvation because they know Jesus at that moment. But if that's all it is—a moment in history—those Christians will find it hard to share their testimony with others. It's difficult to be excited about something that happened years ago, but when a Christian has an intimate, daily, love relationship with the God of this universe, it's not hard to stay excited about and naturally share God's love with others.

Life or Just Forgiveness?

Finally, grace-oriented evangelism offers life, not just forgiveness. Most religions today stress the part of salvation where a person is forgiven of sins so he/she can go to heaven. While that's certainly something to be thankful for, it is not God's primary goal in offering salvation. God's main objective in reaching out to us is to share His life with us.

The churches described in the book of Acts stressed this truth through evangelism, and in a short time the whole known world had heard about Jesus of Nazareth. Today, modern evangelism presents forgiveness, but it generally ignores the aspect of receiving divine life at salvation. Comparing the fervor of the ancient church with today's church makes it clear that omitting this aspect has resulted in a lowered effectiveness of evangelism.

> God's main objective in reaching out to us is to share His life with us.

It was because of our sin Christ died; yet, God offers forgiveness to anyone who receives it. From salvation on, we will never be accountable for our sins because Jesus took them upon Himself: "But God showed his great love for us by sending Christ to die for us while we were still sinners" (Rom. 5:8). That's mercy.

But in Christ we are not just offered forgiveness; we are offered life—joyful, abundant, exhilarating, divine, eternal life: "The thief's purpose is to steal and kill and destroy. My purpose is to give them a rich and satisfying life" (John 10:10). That's grace.

Too many nominal Christians endure mundane lives because their understanding of Christianity revolves around the example set forth by others who follow religion. But when you cast aside the rules and enter into relationship, you can know the true life the God of the Bible offers.

His purpose has always been to bridge the gap between man and God. He wants to have a relationship with you, a personal relationship. In fact, in the Bible, He calls us His bride. It doesn't get more intimate than that. He's not offering a life weighed down with guilt and burdens. He wants you to know and experience the

> Too many nominal Christians endure mundane lives because their understanding of Christianity revolves around the example set forth by others who follow religion.

true life He offers when you enter into a relationship with Him.

Yes, it's true. Jesus hates religion, but He loves you.

Study Questions

1. What are some skills or gifts you believe God has given you?

2. What are some ways that you can get involved in your church so you can exercise those skills?

3. What's the law of love (law of Christ)? How can you practice it this week?

4. List three names of people you know who need to hear about God. What are some of your greatest obstacles in sharing God with them?

Notes

1. C. S. Lewis, *Mere Christianity* (New York: HarperOne Publishing, 1952), 142.

2. See www.drtimwhite.com/2009/11/04/sermon-illustration-on-tad-lincoln.

3. The Revolution, "Raspberry Beret," comps. Prince, 1985.

4. Michael Jackson, "Billie Jean," comps. Michael Jackson, 1982.

5. Strong's G2347.

6. Michael Jackson, "Wanna Be Startin' Somethin'," comps. Michael Jackson, 1982.

7. Steve McVey, *Grace Walk: What You've Always Wanted in the Christian Life* (Eugene, OR: Harvest House Publishers, 1995), 51.

8. Ibid.

9. Ibid., 50.

10. Ibid., 49.

11. Steve McVey, *Finding Freedom & Rest in Grace Land* (Eugene: Harvest House Publishers, 2001).

12. McVey, *Grace Walk*.

13. Steve McVey, *Grace Amazing* (Eugene: Harvest House Publishers, 2001), 84.

14. McVey, *Grace Walk*, 75.

15. Ibid., 110. McVey, *Finding Freedom*.

About the Author

Dr. Alex Himaya is a follower of Jesus, husband, father, pastor, author, speaker, visionary, and leader.

Alex and his wife, Meredith, have four children: Katherine, Eli, Ben, and Lemley.

He is the founding and senior pastor of theChurch.at with campuses at BattleCreek, Midtown, and DuPage. It is one of the fastest growing churches in America. With three campuses, it has grown from 120 to more than 6,000 in its first ten years of existence. theChurch.at is making a difference in Tulsa, America, and the world.

Alex is also the founder of an international orphan care ministry called Adopt(ed).

Alex is a dynamic communicator and leader, obedient to God, and passionate about Jesus Christ, and spreading His Word.